Faith Conscience and Heart

Alastair Fray

Copyright © 2019 Alastair Fray

All rights reserved.

ISBN-13: 978-0-578-47111-2

Editors: Alastair Fray and the Rev. Ron Jones (C&MA)

Scripture quotations are from the ESV® Bible (The Holy Bible, English Standard Version®), copyright © 2001 by Crossway, a publishing ministry of Good News Publishers. Used by permission. All rights reserved

ACKNOWLEDGMENTS

In honor of my wife without whom this book would not be completed. In honor of all those who have loved me so much and invested in me spiritually. In honor of my mom who understood the value of me learning the bible and the gospel of salvation in Jesus Christ even from a young age. In honor of my father and mother who have both sacrificed so that my siblings and I would have good memories and opportunity in life. And last but certainly not least: in honor of the Lord who has extended His mighty hand to me even when He found me in the miry deep who alone is worthy, worthy, worthy of being praised and only reason why I have been enabled to write this book!

CONTENTS

	Acknowledgments	iii
	Introduction	xiii
1	A Subject of Vital Concern	1
	SINCERE FAITH	7
2	The Faith that God Expects from Us	8
3	God's Existence and Character	17
4	The Historical Life, Death, and Resurrection of Jesus Christ	23
5	Concluding Thoughts on Sincere Faith	37
	A GOOD CONSCIENCE	40
6	Introduction to a Good Conscience	41
7	The Magnitude of Our Sin	47
8	My Neighbor is Worse Than Me	61
9	Hero or Villain?	74
10	I'm Worthy of What?	88
11	Conclusion to A Good Conscience	97
	A PURE HEART	101
12	Divided Allegiances	102
13	God of Wealth	108

14	The Idol of Comfort	120
	CONCLUDING THOUGHTS	137
15	Concluding Thoughts	138
	APPENDIX	141
	ABOUT THE AUTHOR	144
	REFERENCES	145

INTRODUCTION

In that the Lord has given me good and meaningful work which he has prepared in advance for me to engage in I have written this book. (Eph 2:10) This book's intent is to directly help those who follow Jesus as Lord, God, and Savior in understanding how to walk in the freedom, peace, and power that is clearly seen in his various disciples as recorded in the accounts and letters of the New Testament. Looking back on my life in wonder at His mindfulness it is amazing and exciting to me that He may so consider my passions and allow me to write a book on gospel obedience. Our spiritual state as those who confess Him as Lord and God and agree that He has risen from the dead began to bother me when I considered such things as a high schooler. Little did I know at that time, being blind in my sin and self-righteous pride, I was on a path leading to becoming one of the most needy and disturbingly sinful human beings that I could ever imagine.

My experience with the Lord God began at a young age reading bible stories with my parents and while attending Sunday morning classes at our church. I read of seemingly superhuman feats of Moses, David, and the Apostles, and learned to respect and have a healthy fear of the Lord. But in looking at the testimony of the power, freedom, and joy in which these people walked despite often violent opposition, and being convinced of their truthfulness, it sparked in me by the grace of God a disgust and sorrow for how shallow an experience of the Lord and his power I saw in the church. Notice though I did not say that it sparked a sorrow or guilty remorse for these things not being present in my own life though I knew little, if anything at all, of this sort of life lived with God at the time. This concern began during my high school years and continued to grow after graduating college. The image I had of myself at the time was one of general obedience to the Lord and I did not suspect anything otherwise. In fact as far as I was concerned I thought myself a model Christian and ready to do the will of the Lord. All the while though I was living a life of selfish ambition, self-righteousness, and committing sin after sin on the inside while keeping things relatively under control on the outside. By the grace of God I was not left on this path. The grace given me was not one I would have ever picked for myself. In 2010 I reached a point of such utter conceit and depravity due to the fruit of many years of sinning instead of walking in faith with the Lord that it shook me unto falling down on my face and begging God for mercy to help me in the midst of a situation that I could not understand at all.

In light of this admitted personal history we must consider my qualifications to write a book on gospel obedience if I am openly admitting that I have been extremely steeped and engrossed in sin. It is in fact precisely the prolonged and difficult process of the Lord lovingly addressing these things in my life as I listened and pursued Him which will allow me to speak meaningfully to those coming out of a similar state. Since all men have sinned and fallen short of the glory of God, and all have turned aside to his own way, one man further trained by the Spirit and Word of the gospel gifted to him may help another who has not made those steps yet. (Rom 3:23; Ps 53:3) I may also say this in another way: that if one man is understanding and familiar with the voice and means by which he has been delivered from the dangers and entanglements he has found himself in he is then empowered and knowledgeable to direct those who currently find themselves in a similar situation. Therefore my qualification to write such things is not by certification of any school or being perfect but by revelation of truth by the same Spirit who dwells in all those whom the Lord has saved, by handling these matters as I have submitted, trusted, and given up fighting Him, and by being familiar with many of the steps God asks us to take to walk in a new life with Him. By this Spirit despised fishermen where made qualified instruments, communicators, and members of the kingdom of God. By this Spirit alone I am qualified to understand and speak about the things of God. My hope and assurance is that the Spirit of the Lord who has lead me out of darkness and bondage into light, peace, wisdom, and power, will be clearly visible in every way. It has been a source of great pleasure and growing joy to experience greater and greater freedom, contentment, assurance, and peace as a result of the Lord working in my life.

It is necessary to clarify a few important things:

1: This book is namely addressed to and intended for those

who already have acknowledged their rebellion, lamented the life of enmity that they have consciously and subconsciously led against the Lord, and have repented by confessing, returning, and beginning to honor Jesus as a good Lord, God, and Savior. Therefore I will be operating under the assumption that many if not all who read this book have heard the word of the gospel: that God the Father has sent His promised Son into the world that we might be saved, forgiven, and reconciled to Him through His death on a cross... and... as He rose again from death, so too we have been born again from the dead unto a new life lived in a newness of relationship with the Lord, apart from sin... and now live in an assurance that we will rise from the grave and live with Him forever in His eternal kingdom versus the hell we deserve. Due to this being the case, certain assumptions may be made knowing that the intended audience will already believe and have a general understanding of certain things. This book and its effectiveness is necessitated upon and assumes that the audience is both born again and has the Spirit of God dwelling in them. I am therefore saying that the effectiveness and further experience of the gospel as a result of the truth of God in this book is necessitated first on that person's Go regeneration and God's Spirit being present in a person's life. This book may help certain unbelievers, as my own doubts, hardness, and guilty ignorance is common to many, but it's true power and intention is to address the state and understanding of those whom have already experienced salvation and are now genuinely seeking to learn how to live and walk with the

Lord.

2: It is necessary to admit that this book is by no means the fruit of me diligently pursuing these truths out of concern for others or those who will read this book but is the result of a fervent concern for my own eternal well-being. In conviction of the truth of judgment, an offer of forgiveness, the arrival of a Savior, the resurrection of Jesus from the dead, the existence and persistent reality of a God who loves us and hates our sin, and in light of my own utterly miserable state, I have pursued the Lord and listened to Him out of concern for my own eternal and present well-being. As I have worked through my own doubts, guilty ignorance, and objections to what He says, while being attentive to what He has said about such things, expecting and receiving the guidance of His Spirit inside me, the following content came to light. In the midst of many, varied, and serious conditions He has faithfully delivered me out of many of them which now allows me to discuss and write about what this process looks like.

3: I therefore am not the Hero of this story, nor could I have hoped to have known any of these things apart from His revealed word and the continued leading of the Spirit of God in my life. I also have been utterly dependent on those who have willingly obeyed His call, loved me, and served me. Again I do not claim to be perfect, but rather, in handling what I have thus far I hope to bless and help those who share similar struggles, sins, and doubts.

4: This book should not be considered a work which

encompasses and includes all areas of progressive sanctification and by no means is a substitute for diligent inquiry, deep consideration, and attentive listening to His revealed word and Holy Spirit.

5: Warning: certain subject matter and arguments may delve into deeper and harder to understand subjects of our faith. This is for two reasons: firstly that this book is not aimed at a narrow but instead wide spectrum of Christians of various maturities and histories and secondly, I have hand-picked subjects of greatest corporate resistance and unhealth in the Church today when it comes to the gospel of Jesus Christ of varied difficulty and depth which I first had to discover by God's grace myself and then remedy by that grace in my own life. These subjects should be understood in the context of the spectrum of mother's milk to steak. Therefore if the reader is choking please take a step back and be circumspect about the reason why: is it because I just hate what is being said or is it because I am not ready to consume this and should be focusing elsewhere? (1 Cor 3:1-2) We are therefore saying that certain subjects may be simultaneously extremely helpful for a relatively mature person grounded and secure in beginnings of our faith or but also unwise and in fact a dangerous choking hazard for an infant in Christ. An infant like any infant should be focused on the necessities: their understanding and faith in gospel and therefore their conviction of the historical birth, life, death and resurrection of Christ, their conviction of who Jesus really is, the beginnings of trust in all members of the Trinity, reading the bible for the first time, and the one, two, or three most important things that Jesus commanded to His disciples. There is no shame in recognizing that one is an infant it is in fact wisdom for to presume otherwise is often both hazardous and foolish... and produces all manner of entanglement. We shall be unraveling many subjects of the Christian faith in the 'milk' category which should not be despised just because they are called milk for they are utterly important, utterly foundational, and are often in fact the fundamental issue that lies behind the disparity between what we currently profess and our actual lives. All these things being admitted... if the reader comes across a subject that is not necessary for salvation and they just don't grasp it or it is not wise for their focus to be on the subject at this time, put a question mark next to the subject, just as I was wisely encouraged in college by one of my mentors to put a question mark next to a verse that I did not understand, and come back to it later. This is wisdom... not resigned failure. Last but not least, we should not be surprised nor frustrated that the gospel can be both simple and immediately receivable but also deep, lengthy, and often difficult when it comes to personal progress and it actually finding root in our lives for our God is both immediately understandable yet infinite, salvation is both simple yet cosmic, men's conditions and spiritual diseases can vary widely, and even the world He has created can be simple at first glance yet have waters that are utterly deep.[1]

CHAPTER 1

A SUBJECT OF VITAL CONCERN

When will we be honest? The visible and audible signs of our sickness are clear to all who look.

Are quarrels, pride, and contempt a crown of honor? Such sound has carried near and far.

How long until we confess that we are weary and still burdened?

    If we are truly honest with ourselves and the reality of our situation as confessing disciples of Jesus Christ we would confess that the gospel and often even the Lord himself have little bearing and are of little consequence in our daily lives. Such things are seen clearly when we consider what consumes our mind daily and is further revealed by our appetites and how closely we resemble our unsaved neighbor: in light of what we esteem worthy pursuing and giving all our life's energy to. Or, if we do not esteem ourselves thus we are often burdened and weary beyond belief. Even worse… many of us as the people of God have settled: acting like limping, striving, and these heavy burdens are both our lot in life and pinnacle of all we can possibly hope for. Therefore I must ask:

    How can this be so?

How can we who confess the turning point of all human history, grounds for the redemption of mankind, the door of eternal life, the resurrection of the dead, heaven and hell, and the means of reconciliation with the God of all the universe be so empty and passionless? Has the gospel failed? Is He powerless to save? Is the life, death, and resurrection of the very Son of God a joke or is it the very "power of God for salvation to everyone who believes" (Rom 1:16)? When dully considered, is it not mind-boggling and exceedingly mournful the obvious disconnect between the lives many of us live before God and the subjects just repeated? Let us therefore once again, in light of the magnitude of the subjects at hand, the potential consequences of treating such things lightly, and in light of the exceedingly great store houses of God's grace, set aside all that our minds are occupied with and even dare I say, even our unceasing religious activity, in order to listen to what the Lord has to say to us:

> Simon Peter, a servant and apostle of Jesus Christ,
>
> To those who have obtained a faith of equal standing with ours by the righteousness of our God and Savior Jesus Christ:
>
> May grace and peace be multiplied to you in the knowledge of God and of Jesus our Lord.
>
> His divine power has granted to us all things that pertain to life and godliness, through the knowledge of him who called us to his own glory and excellence, by

which he has granted to us his precious and very great promises, so that through them you may become partakers of the divine nature, having escaped from the corruption that is in the world because of sinful desire. (2 Peter 1:1-4)

"Having escaped the corruption that is in the world..."? "Has granted to us all things that pertain to life and godliness..."? How contrary do such statements fly in contrast with our current experience, sickly manner, resignations, and excuses!!!??? Sober up then! For this apostle is in fact CELEBRATING at the beginning of this letter! Celebrating in view of the richness and completeness of life which he was experiencing almost 2000 years ago. A life that God granted to him which likewise has been granted to us. (John 3:16) An eternal life to be experienced NOW... "granted to us"... PAST TENSE! Yet in light of this particular word observe one of our potential problems: if something be granted to us we must still seek to lay hold of it or seek to obtain to it... though in the granting the Lord remove all reason to boast should anyone experience the life, power, and grace of it.

Here is the amazing truth and now present reality: He has granted us lives free of fear, driven by purpose, defined by hope, defined by love, defined by power, which can thrive in little or in much, in the calm and in the storm. It is therefore NOT that His plans and decisive victory at the cross have failed to produce His intended results... rather... the precious foundations of our faith whereby we enter and experience the true power, presence, and freedom of His Kingdom are under such a state of disrepair, neglect, and spiritual attack as to undermine the whole new person and create an utterly miserable life of instability.

> Wake up! Wake up! WAKE UP!

Eternal life is not just ahead of us... It has been given to us! His Kingdom is not only coming... but HAS COME!

> Behold! (Look! Understand!) I stand at the door and knock. If anyone hears my voice and opens the door, I will come in to him and eat with him, and he with me. (Rev 3:20)

Let us then, in light of all these things, listen and seek once again with urgency, renewed appetites, and renewed expectation that the power, freedom, peace, rest, and merciful goodness of His kingdom is just as readily available to us today as it was for those who first experienced it some 2000 years ago.

****

All of this begs one vital question: What then have we missed or lost that has led to such a personal and corporate state of disrepair and personal disconnect from the life and power of the gospel? Should we not revisit and reconsider together the words of the apostles?... those that first experienced such things? The apostle Paul understood that which allowed him to walk in freedom, love, and power. He was able to move beyond the good news he received to love others in action, to endure and to suffer, and ultimately to carry this good news unto the far reaches of his world. Consider if individually and corporately as confessing disciples of Jesus Christ we regained such freedom, love, and zeal? The beating heart of the church must come back. We must ask for the grace of desiring it: His present kingdom come into our hearts, minds, activity, and world. Therefore let us listen closely to what the apostle Paul has to say to confessing and regenerated believers who likewise at the time needed to be encouraged. In 1 Timothy 1:5 he explains his present aim toward his readers:

> "the aim of our charge is love that issues from a pure heart and a good conscience and a sincere faith". (1 Tim 1:5)

In looking at the foundations of the new life he is experiencing and living, so contrary to his former, the apostle Paul is singling out three areas of vital importance to their and therefore our spiritual life: A PURE HEART, a GOOD CONSCIENCE, and a SINCERE FAITH. Now if you will permit me to speak to such things... it is our neglect, ignorance, faithlessness, and outright hostility towards the things of God in these fundamental areas which largely account for the sickly manner in which we walk in this world as Christ followers. All of these, I have found, are of vital and interconnected importance to the health of our spiritual lives. My hope by the end of this book is that you will perceive and therefore understand that foundational strength in one of these three categories will affect you and your personal experience of God's eternal life... but one will find over time that each of these are so interconnected... as neglect in one area will still leave you personally limping at best... and at worst... wholly unfruitful and utterly miserable in contrast to experiencing and living in newness and wholeness of life God has granted to us in the gospel of Jesus Christ. We are conflicted. Often divided still between to paradigms, two kingdoms, two mindsets. And would that we set aside all that entangles and hinders us from experiencing this life! For it is something worth our most diligent pursuit! Therefore into these three precious and vital subjects this book will structured: Sincere Faith, A Good Conscience, and a Pure Heart. Unto the intended end that we together fall down and praise the Father, Son, and Spirit for what they have done and unto the intended end that the lame and sick will once again run the hill tops!

SINCERE FAITH

CHAPTER 2

THE FAITH THAT GOD EXPECTS FROM US

It is clear that many of us either do not understand the Lord's call to trust in Him and believe, or, are willfully pretending that the faith to which He calls us will not cost us our sinful ways. The evidence against us is how pale our experience is in comparison with the accounts of the New Testament along with our present proclivity to 'believe'… yet go on living life as if no decisive course of life were required or is the logical and natural outflow of what God has called us to or given us in Christ. Yes… in truth many of us cannot be expected to nor should we personally expect to exhibit the same degree of faith that someone who has physically seen the resurrected Lord would exhibit. But this is not excuse us nor explain our present spiritual state.

Notice in our previous passage of 1 Timothy… the apostle Paul attaches the adjective sincere to the type of faith that leads to love that he wishes us to grasp and practice. He therefore also simultaneously implies that there is a 'false' and 'feigned' faith which we are to be wary of which are an antonyms of the adjective 'sincere'. (1 Tim 1:5) Here is the beginning fact of this matter: people at large, including ourselves, often pretend to an identity and reality which is not true. We are especially adept at seeing this fake front in others, but often are wholly unaware or willfully ignoring it in ourselves. The issue is this: the same is true when it comes to faith and the gospel. **Many pretend to the faith of the gospel... but there is very real disparity between profession and reality.** The reader is therefore firstly is to be reminded when it comes to sincere faith: **that the Lord is looking for us to genuinely trust Him... sincerely trust Him... and not have a faith that is anything less than the faith of the original gospel ... versus lying to ourselves all our lives only to be gravely disappointed on the day of judgment.** As for what we are to confess, trust, or believe on Him for... these things I trust will soon become evident to the reader as the book progresses and the reader gives the attention required.

Our second necessary comment about the sincere faith of the gospel is that it produces children born of God who look and act like Him. "Now I would remind you, brothers, of the gospel I preached to you, which you received, in which you stand, and by which you are being saved, if you hold fast to the word I preached to you – **unless** you believed in vain." (1 Cor 15:1,2) **Observe!** The Apostle Paul himself recognizes that certain people having 'received' the gospel in fact have 'received' it in vain. In other words, it did not produce in them the fruit's of the Spirit, which are the "love, joy, peace, kindness, goodness, faithfulness, gentleness, and self-control" of God. Has therefore the power of God unto salvation failed? Most certainly not! Unless you seriously feel justified in saying that a God with infinite power and all knowledge was not able to devise a sufficient plan to powerfully redeem and save humanity?

Such is both utterly foolish and heinously slanderous. Therefore, to help us understand such things the Lord says to us that some upon believing and then loving God immediately and continuously produce these fruits out of the word spoken to them; others receive the word, are saved indeed, yet "the cares of the world and the deceitfulness of riches and the desires for other things enter in and choke the word, and it proves unfruitful" (Mark 4:1-20); and some should be gravely concerned, because they have received the word, or so they think, but they love and trust him not and continue to live lives that do not honor God or value the cross of Christ at all. The issue then that correlates with the first is that many of us, through pride or often a lack of understanding, pretend to these signs of life lived with God just as I have for many years. (1 Cor 15:1,2; Heb 12:8; Heb 3:12-19)

To hit these images home consider me... for I grew up in the church. For a false understanding of what God desired when He called me to repent led me to believe that what He wanted from me most was to be moral and try hard to obey his commands. For I was aware of His laws and agreed with them. And undoubtedly this mindset is the same in many of those who I would call my brethren who agree with the laws of God but have also never conceived of or experienced the obedience of the gospel: "faith working through love." (Gal 5:6) So. Under the conviction of the reality of a Holy God, the truth of the gospel, the goodness of His laws, and having admitted a 'repentance' of sorts... I tried and lived as morally as possible. But now in hindsight, does this not amount to us making the gospel of the power of God into a moral reformation that anyone can achieve by just agreeing with God's laws and seeking to keep them? Under the conviction of their being a Holy God who loved righteousness and hated evil, I obeyed out of fear... and became exceedingly burdened. For one can obey out of fear for only so long. We have stripped out of our 'gospel' and lost all that makes the true gospel the gospel... something much more than a change of mind toward the keeping morality. The proportion and those things that God values most we have lost sight of. You see... if faith in what Jesus has done on one's behalf does not move to love and instead, what lies behind our obedience to "love the Lord your God with all your heart and with all your soul and with all your strength and with all your mind, and your neighbor as yourself" is our 'trying' to conform to this law as much as we can, then we have still never known and are pretending to the obedience of the gospel without having it's root inside. For faith is the root of obedience. And any other root: fear, pride, and 'trying to be a good person' produce a false or feigned obedience which having no connection to the gospel and therefore the power of God. May the reader then be reminded of what I ultimately had to realize: 'trying' is not faith. Nor does being moral have any mindfulness or admission of a need for the power and salvation of God. For these reasons this book has been written. For on the painful journey of discovery with the Lord out of a place of immense burden and want for but a drop of water in the midst of a valley of death the Lord revealed to me the reasons for why His word was not producing fruit in my life. I had no conception of how to live after salvation... and to be fair... the conceptions that were put forward to me by those within and without the church were wrong, for they too did not know the life of God either.

To those of you who are like me and are easily frightened, fearful, yet responsive when it comes to the warnings of the Lord or a warning that we are to be wary of what 'obedience' we are producing... let us keep in mind that the Lord does save and receive us as sinners. It is often natural for an adopted child, who feels he does not look like his parent, to question and be insecure about if he really is a part of the family. If you have an apparent lack of fruit and don't look like the Lord, but are attentive and responsive to his holy discipline, then he is treating you as a child, and you need not be unhealthily fearful, since you are being treated as his son or daughter. He is faithful to His children. He teaches us to produce fruit when we don't know how. He leads us into the freedom of His obedience out of a valley of death when we are sincere in our pursuit. Discipline will lead to fruit, if you submit to it. It is only the unresponsive and those not being disciplined that have reason to be uneasy.

Thirdly. If so many of us have misconceived life after salvation, what does sincere faith look like? For us to understand this call to sincere faith... what it's like to have the real thing...we must look into the examples of what it is like experientially. For there are many examples of this life in the bible but we misapprehend what God valued in these relationships most. To do so I have chosen among many others the image of our original relationship with God before sin entered the world. In thus approaching our potential understanding , and in also looking at the consequences of our original sin against Him in the garden in the material that follows, it will become much clear what is being asked of us as the sons and daughters of Adam and Eve when we are today told to repent and sincerely "believe".

****

God is a God of order, and this includes the ordering of our relationships. When considering the realities of our original relationship with God in which we were placed, we were created as 'His people' and He is 'Our God'. Just as a king or lord has direct responsibility to love, empathetically care for, and protect his people... and they have grounds to expect that of him... so too were we found in our original state. To compliment this relationship, a king's people also have obligation. Specifically to honor, respect, and give thanks to their king as they have real ground to lovingly trust Him and do lovingly receive and expect things from him in the midst of that trust. Notice he would rightly in turn expect such things of them as their king and lord. What we must revisit and fundamentally grasp once again is that we were originally created in the image of God and for a relationship built on trust, or in other words, faith, with God as our Creator, Lord, and King. The key word here is trust or faith.

Satan, taking opportunity, questioned the goodness of God in the Garden of Eden. And we, despite the evidence and more than sufficient grounds to trust God at His word, doubted that His command had our best interests at heart. (Gen 3; Rom 1:18-23) Therefore. The reason we sinned in Eden and the reason we continue to sin today, is we first and foremost disbelieve that He really is good and has our best interests in mind when He restricts us and instead believe a lie. **The original pollution from Satan Himself, willfully received and believed by us, was a lie leading to sinful doubt, the act of sin itself, consequence, separation, and an inevitable life of fear apart from that relationship which we once shared with God.** (Prv 25:26) In receiving the lie and doubting His good will and heart toward us in the garden of Eden, we justified sin in our mind and that day began looking away from Him to everything and anything but Him. This is called the Original Sin. And it is not just a fairy tale but a persistent reality which explains all manner of activity in this world... for death came through sin, and we, having gone astray, live now quite apart from Him. The Spirit calls this manner of life death, for it is not the unending spiritual life lived with God. (Eph 2:1-10) Key words "life with God"... for sin has separated us from this life and must be dealt with. We are found weary and heavy laden in our pursuits, and the Lord beckons us to return to Him that He would give us rest.

You see, when the Lord, calls us back to Him by using the word 'repent', He is calling a wayward and guilty people back through the window of Christ's death and resurrection to trust in Him once more. Trust in the sense of what we expect in a regained and renewed relationship. The cross therefore is the window of faith. This is the bigger picture of the sincere faith unto which we are called... for it does not only entail forgiveness and the life of Christ, but also reconciliation, restoration, and sure ground for us to trust in the Lord forevermore. In Christ we confess our waywardness, our guilt, and rejoice that He would be willing to forgive us and grant us the gift of an eternal restoration and the grace of walking with Him once again, just as Adam and Eve once walked with Him in the Garden of Eden. Sincere faith then is all about relationship, relationship, relationship... through the window of faith in the good news of Jesus Christ and it's power. Therefore we find that our sight and acknowledgment of that which historically happened before Christ's coming lends to a far clearer understanding of what is needed and what is offered in the gospel of Jesus Christ.

In conclusion then on our first section on sincere faith: it is therefore not for no reason that the apostle Paul lists sincere faith as a vital aspect of our ability to live the new life Jesus bought for us. For just as when we lose a relationship on account of sin on earth, the reader must understand that the offer is not alone forgiveness merely in an accounting sort of sense, but forgiveness in light of a sincere return and prospect of regaining the relationship once lost. We are invited to trust again where doubt and fearful obedience once dwelled. Keeping this reality and fact in mind will shed utterly revealing light, as it has in my life, on the true root of many our sins. But if instead we "let what we heard from the beginning abide in us, then we will abide in the Son and in the Father." (1 John 2:24) The gospel is both the power of God: a restoration of faith, new life, and position that peculiarly addresses and answers our evil doubt as the key to killing the root of sin through a granted new life.

CHAPTER 3

GOD'S EXISTENCE AND CHARACTER

For us to have a sincere faith towards God… we must be convinced that He does exist and that He is of sufficient character to be worthy of our trust for us to believe Him at His word. I can think of no other thing more important which holds together our ability to have a sincere faith in Him. Much good material, evidences, and proofs can be sought out on this subject beyond what I will be including. The evidences and displays of God in scripture testify more strongly and clearly to us about who He is and His existence than anything I could hope to include in this book. Of which, the reader is obligated to pursue in light of them being the very word of God (Heb 1:1-3; 1 Peter 1:12) The greatest of these evidences being found in our last section: The Historical Life, Death, and Resurrection of the our Lord Jesus Christ. One will notice as they inquire into history and other evidences that our faith is not a blind one as some presuppose, but for us to trust the Lord in truth, and live out the life He has given us, our faith must be grounded in an increasing awareness of His existence and unique person, as we learn of Him through evidences, testimonies, the signs He gives us, and experience when once again walking with Him.

****

'Do unto others as you would have them do unto you' said my workmate one day at Starbucks. In the conversation we were having she explained to me that she did not believe in God... but told me that this was the principle by which she lived by and thought others should also. In the midst of this season of my life, the Lord led me to consider her words closer. Unbeknownst to me, the Lord chose to use this conversation as an opportunity to give me further sign of His existence and person, in the midst of a season of doubt and utter instability where I desperately needed assurance. I have chosen this evidence of His person and existence because of the prevalence and agreement among all men of this standard... though this standard be worded and evidence of it's acknowledgment among men, in truth, comes in many forms. Self-contained in this command is the person of God whom we already know. But for us to once again be reminded of this, we must firstly consider what comprises a person.

In John Owen's treatise on the Holy Spirit, he reaches a point where he describes to us the faculties of a person or soul: "the mind, the understanding, and the heart."[2]

There is the mind which:

> "is the leading faculty of the soul; that which looks out after proper objects for the will and affections to receive and embrace. Hereby we have our first apprehensions of all things, whence deductions are

made to our practice."[3]

There is the understanding which:

> "is the directive, discerning, judging faculty of the soul, that leads it to practice. It guides the soul in the choice of those ideas which it receives by the mind."[4]

And there is the heart which:

> "is the practical principle of operation, and so includes the will also. Light is received by the mind, applied by the understanding, used by the heart."[5]

These excellent descriptions, although they may take some time to fully grasp, undoubtedly do describe the faculties of a living person accurately. But... Where do we look to find not only a 'person' but the person of God clearly implied in the command: 'do unto others as you would have them do unto you'?

The reality of how we work is that by the senses given us and the powers of our mind, we are able to look out into our world and receive objects unto our mind... thereby a person "receives" unto themselves that which exists. We then associate names to these objects or things, so that we can describe them to others, since we are social creatures. Reception moves to deduction which moves to understanding... which informs our actions. At some point in time, a person looked out into the world, saw a hairy, four-legged creature, that went "Bark, bark!" and called it a dog. Now, in sight of how a person functions, let us return to the law which my workmate sensed all of us should obey while simultaneously denying God.

For the words 'others' and 'you' to be used at all, these must originate from a person. No other conclusion is rational, since a prerequisite to using these words are the powers of a person to receive that these implied persons exist in the first place, to retain the knowledge of their existence, and willfully communicate them back to 'us' and 'others' in view that we are persons able to receive such things. Yet it is even deeper than this. The word 'do' clearly implies that this person is fully aware of the dimensions in which we live, both space, and time, as 'doing' can only be conceived of in this manner. The word 'unto' implies sight and understanding of more complicated principles such as giving, taking, and accounting. There are even more signs to be found, but for the purpose of not obscuring the main point we will move on. Our first admission what that this law is meant to govern our lives. along with now seeing that it most assuredly comes from a person... that we it in our hearts and see this evidenced in the regular daily assumptions and judgments made in our minds and in our world... we must also admit simultaneously that it both is an authoritative statement and that it expresses their will. These conclusions are what the evidence points to for no other conclusion fits the reality of the universality of my workmates statement nor the daily assumptions and actions we see in men. Meaning: my workmate fully admitted that this was the law that people should live by, and our daily assumptions and judgments, even among those who confess that they have no god clearly show that the universality of this law is reflected our collective expectations. Therefore both admit and show that the burden of human alignment with this moral law does not lie in our decision our societal decision to keep it or not, but that the person we are dealing with, who is the source of this law, is both in a position of power over us and we are obligated to keep His law. Can this not declare the person and character of God any louder?! Therefore the most common law acknowledged among men, that which my workmate admitted while removing God from the equation, clearly leads us to rationally to only on conclusion: the existence of a loving authority, directly implying the historic God of the bible. Let's be honest. People have known and sensed God for centuries, but we have lately come to pride ourselves smarter and above such thoughts, despising and denying the abundant daily evidence before us.

The Apostle Paul also directs our attention to a similar observation about our daily lives by which we can see that we have known Him all along, and know full well of His law.

> Therefore you have no excuse, O man, every one of you who judges. For in passing judgement on another you condemn yourself, because you, the judge, practice the very same things. We know that the judgment of God rightly falls on those who practice such things. Do you suppose, O man—you who judge those who practice such things and yet do them yourself—that you will escape the judgment of God? Or do you presume on the riches of his kindness and

forbearance and patience, not knowing that God's kindness is meant to lead you to repentance? (Rom 2:1-4)

What I would like to draw attention to is that even during Paul's time men rightly judged and in large part knew the will of God, as we continue today. Inevitably, when the Lord reveals the secrets of our hearts and thoughts, we will clearly see that we have known Him all along... therefore why wait until that day? Our judgments, our thoughts, our offense, our expectations, show we know God and know His law, therefore, let's sober up and not be so foolish as to be like the man whom Paul describes, who rightly condemns another's breaking of the law, yet he himself also breaks the law in his own life overtly, or in his hidden heart covertly. It is unto repentance (a sincere return to the God of the Universe) and the kindness of the Lord in the gospel that the apostle directs us, if we find ourselves in such a place. (Rom 2:4) Therefore we know He exists and have clear evidence of both His will and therefore character, our lives invariably reveal this to be so. Hereby we find encouragement to believe the evidences and trust Him... for He does not hide Himself wholly, but is there to be found.

> But from there you will seek the LORD your God and you will find Him, if you search after Him with all your heart and with all your soul. (Duet 4:29)

CHAPTER 4

THE HISTORICAL LIFE, DEATH, AND RESURRECTION OF JESUS CHRIST

There is ONE foundation laid on which all of our faith rests, which is none other than the historical life, death, and resurrection of Jesus Christ and His identity! We as believers should all know this, but more often than not we know very little conviction that such events really did happen. Even among genuine believers, often unbeknownst to us due to a lack of honesty with ourselves, such events are secretly and selectively relegated to the realm of historical fantasy vs authentic history. The resurrection of the dead has become nothing more than a wives tale. But how crazy is that? Since when did the very person of God, the basis of reconciliation, the redemption of man and this world, and the resurrection of the dead become irrelevant? What utterly insane folly! The lightness with which we treat such things, seen in how we can on one day praise God for the gospel but seemingly almost altogether loose sight of such utterly weighty events points to how little conviction or grasp we have of such pressing realities. In contrast was the undeniable reality of such events seared upon the minds of His first disciples which largely explain the vitality, perseverance, and rooted strength with which they upon true conviction lived out the rest of their lives.

I am convinced that many are not so far removed from the almost poor state in which I found myself in. While I personally confessed to believe these things for years and grew up being taught the story, how little conviction I had and how foolishly I led my life I in the disregard of such great things! Until... until the very feeble foundations on which I stood in regards to their authenticity and historicity shook so violently that it threw me into crisis. In this season the Lord, faithful to his promise to me, led me unto multiple resources and servants of His, whom through different avenues and evidences inquired into this vital history and have contributed to clear minded and rational thought toward what historical evidences we do have.

In light of such things, therefore: How can we any longer justify neglecting such things... or is any other subject more deserving of ones attention above these things? Our faith can and will never be sincere as the apostle's were, nor will we ever fully experience in this lifetime the eternal life which He has suffered and died for us for us to experience, until we recognize that it is all not just a story. No... not a story at all! But a gravitational history that consumes all doubts in the light of the truth and draws us inevitably unto one glorious conclusion. So let us as the church and members of the kingdom of God raise the banner high and march backwards so that we can advance forward by the grace and power of God!

Vital Truth

There is one logical place for us to start. The

authenticity of the gospel has long been maligned. Meaning. We have long been bombarded and our faith is maligned in light of this argument:

> The amount of time that has passed and the amount of times the message has passed hands is proof that the gospel message heard today is no longer reliable. It is not authentic. We cannot rely on it!

Is not the very foundation of the heresy of Mormonism built on such ground? And so, with no answer in return, the onlookers scoff or despise the gospel message and leave the word of God… and our once held faith is secretly undermined and it's root in our lives under attack. Admittedly… this argument is plausible. In fact… if the corruption and control of the Catholic church is sprinkled on top and we remain ignorant of the truth it seem a morsel impossible not to both receive and swallow for many. No wonder we lack stability. No wonder we lack the vital strength of grounded faith! But such assumptions could not be further from the truth in light of what we have in our hands.

The above argument of the unreliability of the gospel message thrives in darkness. But darkness or ignorance need no longer thrive, for, God willing, Dr. Komoszewski, Dr. Sawyer, and Dr. Wallace in their book: Reinventing Jesus – How Contemporary Skeptics Miss the Real Jesus and Mislead Popular Culture, have drawn on scholarship, logic, and indisputable statistics to utterly smash the above lie in a flood and "embarrassment of riches"[6]. This embarrassment of riches has to do with how much is in fact available today to textual critics and new testament scholars and the implications of what they find in these texts. Therefore pursue this scholarship and read it if you find this lie rooted, growing, and the source of all manner of instability. In short our attentions are directed by the authors unto us living in the information age. Meaning... we have at our finger tips a wealth of information and ever growing resources which no prior generation could ever imagine. The bible and it's texts being no exception to this rule... the greatest of these present gains for textual critics being the wealth of transcripts of the New Testament and their accessibility for study. And what of this number? "All told, probably between fifteen and twenty thousand texts of ancient versions of the New Testament remain."[7] And "More than one million quotations of the New Testament from the church fathers"[8]. As for what these authors are able to do with such a wealth of information and how they are able to shine irresistible light and logic on the half-truths that permeate our culture about both the reliability of the message itself and acknowledged textual variants, you will have to read for yourself... for the value of their work lies in their experience with the texts and their knowledge of the truth. And for me to quote their scholarship further I fear would not allow them the justice they deserve.

    The point before moving on is this: If you identify one of your spiritual problems as a lack of sincere faith in the authenticity of the message of Christ, that such events and the coming of the Messiah did happen some 2000 years ago... as received by us today.... then pursue valuable scholarship. For the truth is a great remedy for destabilizing and debilitating lies. For this reason many of us have become unstable and weak. For that which we once held as true has come under the fire of debasing lies. And having received such lies we cannot and will not experience the vitality of a granted eternal life until we pull them out of our hearts.

It is worthy of noting before moving on and particularly relevant today to see that, by this scholarship and truth highlighted by the authors, the very foundation on which the heresy of Mormonism is built... the corruption of the gospel message through time necessitating a restoration or new revelation by God and the resulting book of Mormon, is altogether destroyed... and the Holy Bible and the message therein is once again exalted above any other 'gospel' that would pretend and wish to usurp it!

****

Beyond becoming confident in the reliability of the message that we have received, we must also look into the quality of the history recorded which's meaning will become abundantly clear very soon. In this section on the quality of the history recorded and how this ties into sincere faith we will be relying heavily on the scholarship of Sir William Mitchell Ramsay who:

> "by his death (Ramsay) in 1939 had become the foremost authority of his day on the history of Asia Minor and a leading scholar in the study of the New Testament. From the post of Professor of Classical Art and Architecture

> at Oxford, he was appointed Regius Professor of Humanity (the Latin Professorship) at Aberdeen. Knighted in 1906 to mark his distinguished service to the world of scholarship, Ramsay also gained three honorary fellowships from Oxford colleges, nine honorary doctorates from British, Continental and North American universities and became an honorary member of almost every association devoted to archaeology and historical research. He was one of the original members of the British Academy, was awarded the Gold Medal of Pope Leo XIII in 1893 and the Victorian Medal of the Royal Geographical Society in 1906."[9]

Contrary to what one might think, Mr. Ramsay did not begin his studies with a high view of the history presented in the New Testament, namely Acts. But he ultimately became one of the most ardent and relevant supporters of the historicity of the New Testament due to his extensive study, visits, and ultimate expertise in Asia Minor. His scholarship on Acts, the Epistles of Paul, and general observations from a lifetime of study and the consideration of the arguments of his contemporaries are invaluable and particularly effective as a remedy to lies, doubts, and material that masquerades at scholarship... as many of the debasing lies that find root today were not first birthed in this generation, but by our fathers, or even by our father's father. Nor was a word of truth first aimed in response to such things in this generation. The reader is therefore directed toward the growth of coherent thought below from a person more than qualified to weigh in on such a subject as the quality of the history that is recorded in the new testament.

Admitting where he began his study of the history of the new testament and admitting his doubt, he writes:

> I may fairly claim to have entered on this investigation without any prejudice in favour of the conclusion which I shall now attempt to justify to

the reader. On the contrary, I began with a mind unfavourable to it... In fact, beginning with the fixed idea that the work was essentially a second-century composition, and never relying on its evidence as trustworthy for first century conditions, I gradually came to find it a useful ally in some obscure and difficult investigations.[10]

Herein lies the issue at hand. What about the quality of the history recorded in the New Testament? How accurate and truthful are the things that are recorded? Having admitted his clear doubts as his beginning point he then directs our attention toward an objective truth that must be understood: that there is a wide range of histories of various kind and quality:

> There is the history of the second or third rate, in which the writer, either using good authorities carelessly and without judgment, or not possessing sufficiently detailed and correct authorities, gives a narrative of past events which is to a certain degree trustworthy, but contains errors in facts and in the grouping and proportions, and tinges the narrative of the past with the colour of his own time.[11]

> There is, finally, the historical work of the highest order, in which a writer commands excellent means of knowledge either through personal acquaintance or through access to original authorities, and brings to the treatment of his subject genius, literary skill, and sympathetic historical insight into human character and the movement of events. Such an author seizes the critical events, concentrates the reader's attention on them by giving them fuller treatment, touches more lightly and briefly on the less important events, omits entirely a mass of unimportant details, and makes his work an artistic and idealized picture of the progressive tendency of the period.[12]

> The first and essential quality of the great historian is truth. What he says must be trustworthy. Now historical truth implies not merely truth in each detail, but also truth in the general effect, and that kind of truth cannot be attained without selection, grouping, and idealization.[13]

Having admitted the variability of different recorded

histories, his starting point, and the essential qualities that must be present to admit a history being altogether truthful and therefore accurate... what does say about the recorded history of the New Testament through his year of study and visits to Asia Minor?

> It was gradually borne in upon me that in various details the narrative showed marvelous truth.[14]

> The characterization of Paul in Acts is so detailed and individualized as to prove the author's personal acquaintance. Moreover, the Paul of Acts is the Paul that appears to us in his own letters, in his ways and his thoughts, in his educated tone of polished courtesy, in his quick and vehement temper, in the extraordinary versatility and adaptability which made him at home in every society, moving at ease in all surroundings, and everywhere the center of interest...[15]

Before moving on, let it be observed that what he and I wish us to see is that despite where he began, it was gradually borne on him that in various details, the history as recorded, peculiarly belonged in fact to none other than the century that he first believed it pretended to. Remember. It was assumed at his time that the recorded history of namely Acts pretended to the first century, but was a second century composition. As to the varied and many reasons he gives to assign the history and epistles as such, it is for this reason that he composed much of his recorded and readily available scholarship. It is not possible for me to provide the reader with all scholarship and evidences that Mr. Ramsay provides and his journey of discovery. For those are far better read and discovered through his own words. It is therefore up to the reader to responsibly inquire into the many and varied instances that he provides. And why would we rationally not unless we maintain the lie that we are better off not be confronted with the Son of the living God?

Peculiarly his contemporaries also admit to extraordinary accuracy... yet often refuse to admit that the history as a whole should be accepted as true and instead relegate large sections to a history of the second and third rate... and at worst the realm of fantasy. Of such things and his contemporaries thoughts, for the purpose of sorting through their varied and contrary views for his own sake and clarity of mind, he writes these various, valuable, and progressive thoughts:

> They recognize many of the signs of extraordinary accuracy in his statements; and these signs are so numerous that they feel bound to infer that the facts as a whole are stated with great accuracy by a personal friend of St. Paul.[16]
>
> How does it come that a writer, who (apparently) shows himself distinctly second-rate in his historical perception of the comparative importance of events, is able to attain such remarkable accuracy in describing many of them? The power of accurate description implies in itself a power of reconstructing the past, which involves the most delicate selection and grouping of details according to their truth and reality, ie according to their comparative importance.[17]
>
> It became more and more clear that it is impossible to divide Luke's History into parts, attributing to one portion the highest authority as the first-hand narrative of a competent and original authority, while regarding the rest as of quite inferior mould. If the author of one part is the real Luke, or any other person standing in similar close relations with the circle surrounding the apostles (particularly Paul), then that same person must be the author of the whole, and must have brought to bear on his whole work the same qualities which made one part so excellent.[18]
>
> We might ask whether it is a probable or possible view that the author can

be so unequal to himself, that in one place he can show very high qualities as an accurate historian, and that in another place, when dealing with event equally within the range of his opportunities for acquiring knowledge, he can prove himself incompetent to distinguish between good and bad, true and false. He that shows the historic faculty in part of his work has it as a permanent possession.[19]

Acts, as Lightfoot pictures it, is to me an inconceivable phenomenon; such a mixture of strength and weakness, of historical insight and historical incapacity, would be unique and incredible.[20] But it must be said that this way of reasoning is really mistaken and unjustifiable: it refused to make the inference that necessarily follows from the first admission.[21]

His strength in the details implies his authorities, as well as the strength in the story he is relaying.

That Paul believed himself to be a the recipient of direct revelations from God, to be guided and controlled in his plans by direct interposition of the Holy spirit, to be enabled by the Divine power to move the forces of nature in a way that ordinary men cannot, is involved in this narrative. You must make up your minds to accept or to reject it; but you cannot cut out the marvelous from the rest, nor can you believe that either Paul or this writer was a mere victim of hallucinations. The marvelous is indissolubly interwoven – for good or for bad – with this narrative, and cannot be eliminated. Do the marvelous adjuncts discredit the rest of the narrative, or does the vividness and accuracy of the narrative require us to take the marvels with the rest and try to understand them?[22]

And here we come to the crux of the progression and growth of his logic and collective observations: that though his contemporaries do admit to extraordinary signs of the history in its details leading them to "feel bound to infer that the facts as a whole are stated with great accuracy by a personal friend of St. Paul", they are still relegating large sections to the realm of second rate, third rate, and historical fantasy and therefore have "refused to make the inference that necessarily follows from the first admission." Which is this: that "His strength in the details implies his authorities, as well as the strength in the story he is relaying." We, even as Christ followers, know all too well how hardened we can be when it comes to facing the light of the truth. We therefore are to listen to Heb 3:12 and "Take care, brothers, lest there be in any of you an evil, unbelieving heart, leading you to fall away from the living God." We are not to be like the majority of Israel, who being delivered out of slavery in Egypt by the blood of a lamb, despite wonderful signs of God's power and promise toward them, did not believe nor have sincere faith in the promise… but coveted their former life and turned backwards in their hearts. We must therefore not follow in the footsteps of those who have likewise looked straight at the truth or and refused to believe. For despite our fears, and our proclivity to value our former lives above that which He brings to us, we will find He in truth is "gentle and a servant at heart and we will find rest for our souls" if we overcome our doubt and leave our past behind. (Matt 11:29)

Furthermore, rational consideration within the context of the first century and that time which followed and a view of those evidences we have from this point in history and are very profitable indeed!:

- The crucifixion of Jesus as a clear sign and obvious deduction of "state sponsored terror": ie persecution from Jews who did not receive Him nor believe the message of God. The accounts of both the Roman state and Jews saying "don't follow this man".
- Nero's blaming of Christians in July of AD 64 for the fire in Rome and the community's subsequent persecution.
- Proscription of the name within 50 years of death by Emperor Domitian. Meaning that if you were found to be a Christian, it could cost you your life.

- Pliny the Younger's accounts to Emperor Trajan around AD 112 of Christians who had been given the chance to renounce Christ and worship the Emperor, but chose death over fear and denying Christ.
- The extensive writings of the Jewish historian Josephus, 37 – c. 100, which support the historicity of the specific people, culture, and events of the Gospel, Acts, and the Epistles.

Let us therefore reason together. If the life, death, and resurrection of Jesus Christ was nothing but a hoax, or a carefully constructed story with ulterior motives, or a weak renegade sect of Judaism, how can we explain both the growth and perseverance of it's converts in the face of such overwhelming and violent opposition? If it were but a hoax do you honestly believe anyone involved in the hoax would die for such a thing? Or if a carefully crafted story can anyone rationally believe those closest to the proposed history of events would to die for that which did not even happen? Or have we forgotten that this history involves specific historical peoples, huge public gatherings in and around major cities, and admitted events of importance spanning across the Roman Empire? If it were but a weak renegade sect of Judasim how can you explain it's vitality and persistence despite such obvious and implied violent opposition? Of which level of conviction of the resurrection of the dead and ones standing with God must one have to… in the face of death not deny Christ, which are the plain and recorded observations of Pliny the Younger when interrogating those who are accused simply for being Christians? To relegate all 1st and 2nd century Christians as mad men is to be utterly ignorant and in complete denial of even the most basic evidences present before us. To take our distant ancestors and label them all a bunch of superstitious fools... is not this complete ignorance as well nor being honest or circumspect about the intentional conversation, careful study, reasoning, and, most of all, explosion of excitement we find in the writing of the Apostles and 1st century disciples. Is it not instead men and women who no longer fear death and can rationally look with utter assurance unto God for what He has promised them that alone can act and persevere in such ways? Which begs the question, what gave them such utter boldness in the face death? Of the early church, in the context of all his accumulated knowledge of the historical context and circumstances of these points in history, Mr. Ramsay says thus: "The difficulties in which the Church was placed, which would have killed a weakly life, only stimulated its vigor and its creative energy."[23] The evidences all point one direction: the nature of the conversation, the excitement seen by multiple authors and obvious implication of many others being involved, the rapid spread of Christianity seen in scripture and clearly implied for Nero to even chose Christians as a scapegoat in AD 64. But most of all... the martyrdom and perseverance of Christianity in the face of such overwhelming violent opposition is sure evidence to how monumental of an event and Person that they first and we too are wrestle with. This is no small conviction! It is none other than the life, death, and resurrection of Jesus Christ of Nazareth, promised in various ways through many God ordained means throughout history, an all-consuming message of faith, hope, and love for all men! Praise Him! Praise Him! Praise Him!

****

The context of what is known about early church history through scripture and outside of scripture and rational deductions made in light of knowing human fears and tendencies, since we are also human, rules out so many foolish lies and ridiculous theories about the origins of Christianity that masquerade as scholarship. Of this history: the authenticity of the original message and it's quality... we have talked about sufficiently at this point for us to tie much of what has been said in this vital opening section on sincere faith. There is much more to mine out of general consideration and meditation on the evidences and facts we have in hand. If you are interested in specific examples of the "marvelous truth"[24] Ramsay was so excited to find which changed his mind to list Acts, Luke, and the Epistles in the category of "historical works of the highest order"[25], pursue and read about these things. Historical documents, scholarship, and our accessibility to these things are unprecedented in this age of the internet and public domain material.

CHAPTER 5

CONCLUDING THOUGHTS ON SINCERE FAITH

To remind the reader, we have at this point expressed these things about the sincere faith of which we are concerned: that it leads to holiness, we have looked at a fuller picture of the manner of faith he is calling us to through the lens of our original relationship with God and what happened at the point of original sin, we have highlighted the utter importance of a growing awareness of his existence and character, and we have ended with the indispensable historical events of the birth, life, death, and resurrection of the Lord Jesus Christ. Revisiting where we started, we said that in the Apostle Paul directing our attention toward the subject of sincere faith, he also simultaneously implies that there is a feigned or false faith. In light of all we have now talked about we can better see ourselves and understand if we have been lying to ourselves. Is my faith producing the genuine fruit of the gospel? Does my faith resemble the faith that He has called us all to? Am I assured of His character as to be able to begin to trust Him? Am I sure of His life, death, and resurrection or have I been deceiving myself? It is for these reasons that I have wrote this book, that the foundations of the life that we have been given by the living God be clearly perceived, attended to personally in our lives, and we all attain to as full of a life lived before His awesome return. Of what strength of life would we expect from a person who has little conviction of His existence? What degree of instability would we expect in the one who is not fully sure of His character? How can we ever face danger and look beyond this life if we possess so little conviction of the historicity of His life and have not perceived the signs of His historical resurrection from the dead? I know this is where many of us stand, for it is where I have found myself, even after many years of attending church. Let us not fear to come close to Him, for you will find that what He gives is what you have always been looking for, and what He asks you to leave behind, pales in comparison to what you have found.

In light of such things and such discussion, are we now together beginning to see what a root of instability and lifelessness doubt can be? It is very profitable for us to know that doubt was the original root of sin and continues to be today... for then we appreciate God's particular gift and remedy by sincere faith restored in the good news of His Son. How will we receive once again God and be rid of our doubts but by true conviction that He lives and all that was said about His Son is true and has happened? There is no other remedy to our doubts other than the good news of Jesus Christ and the person of God. God peculiarly seeks to plant this mustard seed in our hearts that it grow, it's roots run deep, and it peculiarly remedy all the sinful doubt's and slanders the Spirit finds in our hearts which we harbor against the word of truth. We must be honest with ourselves and not pretend to a reality of faith before others that neither resembles nor has root in historical faith. For the stakes are far too high... and the eternal life granted to us today and forevermore far too great... for us to be content with a lie.

As a reminder, we are in pursuit of the power of the Gospel of Jesus Christ and what the Apostle Paul wants us to perceive and practice when he says a 'sincere faith' is one of three important bases on which our love for God and others is built. Our faith, for it to truly be a 'sincere faith' that affects and transforms us, must be grounded in the most fundamental historical tenants of Christianity. To us today, the life, death, and resurrection of Jesus can become a distant reality which seems to have little meaning or bearing on our lives some 2000 years after the fact. But if we read anew the testimonies of Jesus's disciples in settled assurance and view of their integrity, the story at hand finally lays claim to the realm of historical reality, extreme importance, and timeless relevance. A reality, message, and power that transformed fishermen and enemies into disciples, who then spread the good news unto the reaches of their world in the face of great dangers, over a lifetime, and unto their often painful deaths. **For us to sincerely believe and experience the power of the kingdom of God in our lives, we must grasp anew the reality that these men and women were utterly convinced of: the life, death, and resurrection of the God man, Jesus Christ.**

A GOOD CONSCIENCE

CHAPTER 6

INTRODUCTION TO A GOOD CONSCIENCE

Similar to sincere faith, our next appeal is to another part of our person: our consciences. Our lack of a good conscience in God's sight is particularly significant reason amongst the three for our poor spiritual experience. On top this, it is most assuredly the underlying spiritual issue leading to particularly vile symptoms apparent in us individually and in the church today and therefore this subject deserves our immediate and undivided attention. For! … Undeniably the gospel fundamentally and directly appeals unto our consciences. Therefore most assuredly this being the case… we must answer this question: wherein lies the dividing line between a good conscience inside a man and an evil conscience inside him? For the apostle most certainly fervently desires us to perceive the contrast. Otherwise he would not have made a point of bringing it up. Therefore it is unto this dividing line we will be directing our attention… unto the end that we see what we have secretly been hiding from even ourselves and unto the end that we both individually and as the church regain sight and knowledge of to what degree and whether either of these mindsets exist inside of us. Therefore in an a Spirit guided effort to convey a clear picture of a good conscience we will in fact be dwelling on it's opposite, an evil conscience, for a large amount of our time so that the reader can receive and understand both realities.

****

"Sons of the devil?" "Deserving of death?" "Dead in trespasses and sins?" "Deserving of eternal punishment in hell?" If we are truly honest, even we as born again believers continue to choke on many of the things that the Word of God says about us, just as I secretly did for many years. Examples of an evil conscience are manifest in denying guilt, blaming God, and saying or secretly thinking things such as: "I'm a pretty good person" apart from the saving grace and power of the gospel. But how odd and contrary is it for the believer to both agree with God yet still be at odds with Him? So we often find ourselves... even as born again believers. The gospel reality that explains this dual reality is this exceedingly great news: that quite despite our hardness or full agreement with all He has spoken to us the Lord knows when a heart is genuine in response to the call of the gospel to repent and believe in His gospel message and therefore He does not a perfect admission of our spiritual bankruptcy nor a perfect understanding of the cross for us to be received by Him and experience His salvation. Is this not exceedingly great news!!?? For instead, He is readily and patiently waiting to receive us again unto himself even with, and especially with: our baggage, our sin, our hurts, and... don't miss this... even with the remaining hardness of our consciences to what He has said. Therefore. Yes! Many of us have firm ground to believe and be confident He has graciously received us and will continue with us. But! He most certainly will not be content as a Father with us continuing to selectively hold to a childish mind of enmity or unbelief.

It is necessary that we are crystal clear. Those who have experienced salvation: the hardness's, the resistance that remains, or our continued lack of agreement with God… these are the tangible and experiential symptoms of our old and evil conscience that remain in part and war against our new person so that we "do not do what we want to do, and we do what we do not want to do" even after salvation. (Rom 7:15-25). Such things are to be put to death (Rom 8:13). Yet how this is done is largely untaught and remained an enigma to me for an exceedingly long time. By the grace of God this is no longer the case! We will get to together see both God's provided means and our active part in applying those means which is God's design.

The often unrecognized truth therefore is that we even as disciples often harbor inside of us the remnants of a heart that is still at odds with Him. We agree with Him not. WE HONESTLY DON'T AGREE! The time is now for us to realize that merely knowing the doctrines of scripture is not enough! It is only in seeing these doctrine's truthfulness and only in sincere instead of feigned admission that such things as death and hell belong to us personally where we will recover the joy, power, and abundant life seen in His first disciples. It is in true agreement with the gospel message alone where our evil conscience will change unto a good conscience.

****

Before delving into few select areas of greatest resistance to the gospel message by our consciences that I have intentionally chosen amongst a much larger pool, and as a necessary introduction to remind and enlighten us to our inner persons, it will do us a great deal of good to firstly consider a few vital details related to a ever growing view of the of sin through the perfect eyes of the Lord.

We as confessing believers, often focus on what the Lord tells us to not do, which is fine and all... but this turns out to be a very narrow minded glimpse of the law of God and how much of our lives are to be submitted to Him. In fact this view, if we really consider it, far more resembles the world's view than any image put forth by the Lord. In truth, my 'obedience', my focus used to be on these prohibitions, and, in believing I was keeping them this mindset inevitably resulted in enormous self-righteous pride in my heart, as it progressively does in many. The law of God does in fact prohibit certain actions such as idolatry, murder, and sexual immorality, but we must also understand that it also gives us positive commands about what to do, such as loving God and loving our neighbor. Therefore we can sin by commission or omission: commission being when we do what we are not supposed to do, and omission being when we do not act as we are supposed to. Therefore take heed of this: IT IS SIMPLY NOT ENOUGH to merely avoid certain sins... there are positive commands which the Lord gives us as well which are required of us. And they are required indeed:

> Do not think that I have come to abolish the Law or the Prophets; I have not come to abolish them but to fulfill them. For truly, I say to you, until heaven and earth pass away, not an iota, not a dot, will pass from the Law until all is accomplished. Therefore whoever relaxes one of the least of these commandments and teaches others to do the same will be called least in the kingdom of heaven, but whoever does them and teaches them will be called great in the kingdom of heaven. For I tell you, unless your righteousness exceeds that of the scribes and Pharisees, you will never enter the kingdom of heaven. (Matt 5:17-20)

Yet, the law of God goes even deeper than this. The law of God is meant to control not only our outward person, but the inward person of our heart:

> And he said, "What comes out of a person is what defiles him. For from within, out of the heart of man, come evil thoughts, sexual immorality, theft, murder, adultery, coveting, wickedness, deceit, sensuality, envy, slander, pride, foolishness. All these evil things come from within, and they defile a person." (Mark 7:20-23)

In saying these things the Lord is clearly pointing to the heart as being the literal fountain from which all our outside actions flow from. Truth be told, we often choose to form our self-image, our very identities, on the type of person we maintain outwardly, often, all the while ignoring our inner person. In saying these things the Lord reminds us of what we already should know: what I speak and what I act first starts inside of me. If I am murderous, it may not ever reach my hands, but the Lord sees my heart. If I am covetous and adulterous, I may never act on such things, but the Lord sees my heart. The list of things we commit in our hearts and evil conversation we conduct there is exceedingly long indeed. Some exhibit self-control over their evil hearts and filter what comes out, while others act openly on this evil principle, yet, we must understand that both people have evil in their hearts. Therefore one murders on the outside, while another feels nothing but cold hearted indifference or contempt towards certain people and groups in their heart, which is murder of the heart. (Matt 5:21, 22) The point in all of this is that our heart is the principle person. Therefore it is not just our outside actions that are to come under the control of the Lord, but also our hearts. Having begun this conversation now, we will be revisiting it later in the midst of this much larger section, when we are given the grace of considering a far deeper and more eye opening view of how the Lord sees our sin. But our beginnings shall be elsewher

CHAPTER 7

THE MAGNITUDE OF OUR SIN

If I ate an apple from a tree which I was not supposed to eat of and the punishment was spiritual death, ultimately culminating in physical death and eternal punishment in hell, one would think that the judge is especially incapable, if not outrageous, when it comes to prescribing a correct punishment to fit the crime. Yet we know that God is perfectly just, all knowing, and sees actions and circumstances for what they are. Therefore, if we aren't bent on slandering Him, are we missing something? Beginning here, the first question then must be, to answer and address the overt objections of our consciences to what the Word of the Lord speaks to it is this:

> Of what are we guilty as to justly deserve such an inconceivably horrible punishment?

To begin this inquiry, let us reflect on the first major section of this book and remember that God created us as His people, which carries with it certain expected responses and obligations... as He, quite apart from any individual choice or opinion, is both our Lord and our God. In making us in His image, He gave us a mind, knowledge, and power to perceive who He was and is and forever will be in relation to us, along with an ability to perceive His character. In doing this, we were and continue to be without excuse when we question His character and believe the lie that He isn't good. But what do we mean in saying that we question His character? Observe that children are in fact also created and born into an existing relationship with their parents where apart from their individual choice or opinion in the matter, placed upon them are certain expectations and obligations due to the nature of their relationship. This leads us to a familiar yet spiritually lost image of relational sin that we must absolutely again grasp if we are to regain health and understand what the Lord has been communicating to us all along. When a child willfully chooses to reject the word of their parent, such as not coming home by curfew time, their actions speak to what their mind is thinking, even though their mouth may be silent: "I think I know better than you"… "I don't trust you"… "I have no respect for you"… "I don't think you have my best interest in mind"… and the list may go on. Observe that the actions of the child directly slander their parent who most often does love them and does have their best interest in mind, and thereby they sin against them by not giving to them the respect they deserve. Saying that the parent deserves respect directly implies that there are certain qualities of theirs, when objectively considered, that should not just be passed over but rather esteemed from their children. Qualities which they possess that should prompt us to listen are their wisdom, their experience, their knowledge, their value, their position, their authority, their character, and this list may go on as well. I fully understand and acknowledge that not every parent to child relationship fully images what we are getting at, but the brokenness and sinfulness that may distort a true image of health between the two has not so distorted this relationship or our other relationships as we cannot fully apprehend and receive this point. Therefore to understand the depths of our sin against Him, with our relational experience in mind, we will firstly be seeking to answer: what qualities of God do we namely slandered when we sin against Him?

Slander No 1: The Lord's Love and Character

The Lord's love for us is perfect and is best expressed in the gospel message of Him coming to seek those who have gone astray from Him, and it further expressed in the gospel gift of eternal life where we return to Him through repentance and His Son to enjoy a faithful and overwhelmingly generous love with Him for all time. His love is also displayed to us in creation, in that He has given us things that bring us joy and pleasure. Thereby the photographer takes pictures and can make a living. Thereby the chef combines flavors which people savor. Thereby we enjoy the relationships and things He has given us. Yet despite all these evidences of His love for us, we reject His wisdom and commands, directly and publicly drawing into question His character and love for us. It is of the utmost importance for us to consciously stop and dully recognize this... that without a doubt the more reason and grounds for us to believe in God's love for us, the worse it is when we choose to set aside these evidences and doubt His character. If I put far too little trust in a person I've known for a week, they are slandered, but you may not be at all that angry with me. If I fix a spying and wary eye on my wife who has only shown faithfulness, excitement for me, and evidences of her excellent character to me all my life, I've treated her far worse, and you'd be rightly outraged at me in light of the greater weight of evidence to the contrary. The truth of the matter when it comes to God is that we have been given unequivocally greater testimonies and evidences which display His character: all of creation, every good thing I've ever enjoyed, every bite of good food I've had, every experience that has brought me joy, the evidences of scripture, the good news of Jesus Christ, the resurrection of the dead, all the fulfilled promises and prophecies of God, and the list must go on and on! And here is where things get exceedingly serious. When we... despite the immense weight of evidence to the contrary, believe and hold to lies about His character, we participate in a monstrous, single, and continual slander in holding to and openly questioning a perfectly good God. We may not openly say the words that He is a liar and not good, but out actions speak volumes to the contrary. He has given us and myself an immense weight of evidence and perfect display of His love to believe, to currently behave, and to have behaved otherwise. Therefore, STOP! ... and consider these questions until you profit from them!:

> 1: How great and many are the evidences of His character He has given us to trust Him?

> 2: In consideration of greatness and multitude of these evidences of His love, how great and many are the reasons he has to be outraged in that we have slandered Him so?

Yet... He is patient, understanding, and longsuffering in the face of such slanders, and in the face of even greater heights of sinfulness, as we will see as we continue our investigation into being honest and knowledgeable about our relational sin.

Slander No 2: "I Know Better."

Is there a more common expression of pride than foolish disregard in the face of obvious experience, knowledge, and wisdom? Thereby a student spouts their opinion in opposition to their qualified teacher, on a subject they have barely handled. "I know better". Thereby a teenager chooses a woefully painful and destructive path, despite repeated warnings from their parents and peers who know the road leads to trouble, pain, and separation. "I know better". Thereby we chose our own way, apart from the straight path of faith, life, relationship, and peace, which the Lord has set before us. "We know BETTER!" Similar to our previous illustration, notice that as the weight of experience, knowledge, and wisdom of a person increases, the greater possible sin and assumed guilt when we foolishly disregard their words. Consider then, what is the breadth, height, and depth of God's knowledge and wisdom? To what extent is it's limits?

> For the Lord gives wisdom; from his mouth come knowledge and understanding (Prv 2:6)

> The Lord by wisdom founded the earth; by understanding He established the heavens; by His

knowledge the deeps broke open, and the clouds drop down the dew. (Prv 3:19,20)

He changes times and seasons; he removes kings and sets up kings; he gives wisdom to the wise and knowledge to those who have understanding (Dan 2:21)

Stop everything! How closely then should we listen?

Do we not give ear and go to great lengths to listen and discuss those whom we esteem? Yet His word is gathering dust and we would rather listen to any and every voice but His. This reflects and shows how outrageous we have become. Lord forgive us for so great a disregard of Your awesome person! We first have doubted His love for us leading to a profane disregard of the awesomeness of His knowledge and wisdom. Such disregard is mind boggling foolish and an utter evil. Yet He is still patient, understanding, and longsuffering in the face of such things… though the picture is unfortunately exceedingly worse:

Slander No 3: "Your Authority is Nothing to Fear"

The Lord says this to Adam, after he had watched his wife eat of the tree and then ate of it himself: "Because you have listened to the voice of your wife and have eaten of the tree of which I commanded you 'You shall not eat of it' cursed is the ground because of you." (Gen 3:17a)

What need to get straight is when we sinned against the Lord in the garden of Eden we rebelled and disregarded the direct command of the Lord our God... as we continue in today. Most of us are not ignorant of His laws... but even if we are without, observe that those without the law of Moses or words of Jesus Christ, despite their lack thereof, often keep and respect these commands to the best of their ability, showing that God has written His law on all our hearts, and thereby show they too are without excuse. (Romans 2:14, 15) One rebels' against the commands of the law, another against the command of the gospel, and yet another the commands on his heart. Rebellion is namely what the Lord chooses to single out and speak unto our first parents, let us then consider rebellion in degrees. (Gen 3:17-19)

The titles Lord and God directly imply to us a certain degree of authority. My manager at work sits in a seat of power over me. The President of the United States sits in a seat of even higher power over me. And, ultimately, the Lord sits in the highest seat above me, exercising infinite and ultimate power over me and all things, as his name directly implies and necessitates... since, to be God is to have nothing above you. What we namely need to see and once again be reminded of is... the more power that an authority exercises the worse it is when I have no regard or correct fear and trembling for that power which they wield over me. Just think of how foolish it looks and evil it is when teens treat their superior with such utter disregard and contempt. What if that authority was over all the cosmos, every atom, every outcome? What degree of respect would He rightly feel entitled to in light of the awesomeness of His power? And what if we did not give that to Him at all in light of our complete lack of respect and healthy fear when we singularly or continually disregard His command? An infinite power is deserving of infinite respect. Contempt and disregard for an infinitely respectable person who wields such power cannot be but an infinitely big sin. Yet He is longsuffering with us even still? For Adam and Eve were not incinerated, nor thrown into an eternal prison. No! Instead we confusedly find the Lord seeking them out, pursing them quite despite their actions, in hope and love, as He continues this day... pursuing the wayward sons of Adam and Eve... lifting them out of and putting away their shame through the shame of the cross, just as we peculiarly find Him in the garden first graciously covering the shame of our parents with clothing crafted of His own hands!

All of us are without excuse. As we have been reminded earlier, His person has been clearly displayed to us: by His creation (Rom 1:20), by His commands that are written on our hearts (Rom 2:1-2,14-15), and by other evidences He has provided (Heb 1:1-5). And all of us have not honored Him nor given thanks as we should. (Rom 1:21) The point is that we apprehend and appreciate both the severity of our sin and greatness of God's grace and mercy. Only in light of such things do we begin to understand the horrific debt that we owe God due to the implied evil we have caused Him, and only then do we begin to understand and truly appreciate the infinite worth of Christ's blood freely given to pay God's and other's legitimate claims against us.

In view of seeing Him far more clearly once again through a consideration of His revealed person, we begin to understand anew why He was described by our forefathers as being "Holy, Holy, Holy" above all other possible ways of describing Him. (Is 6:3) While we share certain attributes with God by His design, the Lord is still nonetheless altogether awesome and different than us; and therefore more worthy of respect, healthy fear, and trust than any other thing or person we could give it to... and in not giving Him this respect in light of how deserving He is of it, we are guilty of an unimaginably huge sin, for again... a lack of respect or flat out apathy for an infinitely great and awesome God is an infinitely horrific sin, of which there is no end to His reasons to be angry with us.

> "Yet even now," declares the Lord, "return to me with all your heart, with fasting, with weeping, and with mourning; and rend your hearts and not your garments." Return to the Lord your God, for he is gracious and merciful, slow to anger, and abounding in steadfast love." Joel 2:12, 13

Yet even now, what we have thus just discussed thus far most certainly speaks to the magnitude of our sin does not fully explain Adam and Eve's sin since rebellion is not and cannot merely be explained by looking at degrees of authority.

Rebellion Continued – A Violation of a Trust

We thus far have been given the grace of talking about

and seeing increasing degrees of disrespect and rebellion with their apex sin being committed in light of a clear display of God's love, knowledge, wisdom, and power. But is there more? Have we missed something? Has something been plainly before us, expressed over and over by the Lord, yet tragically unappreciated by us?

We have indeed lost sight of something exceedingly great. This missing piece is found in that the offense of rebellion cannot be explained merely by a disregard of real power or authority plainly understood and displayed to us. In the midst of studying and asking the Lord for His gracious help and depending on the Spirits answer on matters seemingly unrelated in my mind to our present subject I was reminded of this:

Our relationships are characterized by varying degrees of trust... from the trust between us and a casual acquaintance to the trust we give another in the midst of our most intimate and longest lasting relationships. In addition, there is various ground on which we extend our trust to others... meaning the more sure or stable the ground perceived for trusting another, the more we can entrust ourselves to another. The reader having grasped what has preceded... let our focus now shift to the word "entrust". For consider with me and be reminded by our Lord: What we really mean when we say we trust another is that we are willing in degrees to entrust them with ourselves and with what is ours. Therefore I may entrust 10$ to a casual acquaintance with the expressed expectation that I will need that money back, but I most certainly won't entrust them with my child, for there is not a basis there or justification that affords me to rationally do so. We must add one last thing to the picture though if we are to reach a truly vital and clear image that leads to us seeing that which we have lost sight of. The last thing being this: The varying grounds on which we trust 'afford' us something. In Merriam Webster's words on the word 'afford': these grounds "make available, give forth, or provide naturally or inevitably"[26] something. But what is that something?

The prerequisite to us trusting another is a sense of safety. Is not a sense of safety needed to entrust ourselves? For we must be reminded at this point in history of a simple fact that we in the back of our minds already know… that to entrust ourselves to another is also to expose ourselves. For though we may knowingly and increasingly make available our belongings through trust… or even entrust our person, our emotions, and our bodies to another… there is a recognition that we must be afforded various degrees of safety to rationally do so… lest upon exposing ourselves… our trust be violated. Are you following me? We're almost there! Now us pulling this all together:

Yes. Increasing trust is something that we feel. But in saying that our trust has been violated cannot simply be explained by our loss of those feelings that we previously had and a justified sense of being guarded. No… we must recognize that something else that we have a sense of but often cannot explain is going on. We are taking something of recognized value of ours and entrusting it to another.

Maybe think of the word trust in a monetary sense. The greater the recognized value of the thing being entrusted, the greater grounds needed to feel safe to give it in the first place. The danger or exposure being that we are taking increasingly valuable belongings and even our very emotions, lives, or person and are entrusting that they will both be valued and respected. The greatest earthly image of this being when we are encouraged by the Lord to reserve ourselves, our emotions, our heart, our bodies for the one we will marry, and on that day, entrust ourselves to that person that we will be received and respected as the greatest of earthly gifts that they could ever receive. But not flippantly... or lightly...but under the greatest of promises, an oath, where the Lord both implies the value of the gift being received and, in honor of our own need for sure ground and safety when it comes to entrusting our own self wholly to another. But how does this lengthily reminder to us about trust and entrusting, grounds, and the safety afforded have to do with the cross, original sin, the magnitude of our sin, and the reason why Christ himself needed to die in our place? Let's pull it all together.

We need to be reminded that God too is a person. His personhood and our creation in relationship with Him as His people and Him as our God are what all of a sudden bring all that has just been discussed into play. For thereby He informs us that we trust but He also trusts. We entrust and He also entrusts. We have ground that affords us safety and... DON'T MISS THIS... He has ground that affords Him safety. For we have forgotten that before the fall, He had entrusted Himself unto us. Gave Himself to us freely as a gift to received and lived with faithfully. But we rejected the gift and rebelled against the relationship. And therein lies the horrific and central sin that sent Jesus to the cross... for to reject a perfect display of love is horrible indeed... and the disregard and disrespect of perfect knowledge and wisdom horrific... and rebellion against a command from an infinite authority horrific... but to reject God himself is as personal and as big as it gets. For firstly the sin cannot be more intimate... for we should fully know that personal rejection in the face of utter exposure is as personally offensive as it gets and wounds deeply. And secondly. Who can place a price tag or come up with a value on what was rejected? Or of what value can He not but consider himself to those He created, gave life, surrounded with blessings, and freely offered Himself to through relationship? God does not hold back... neither in the gospel... nor did He hold anything back at creation... for... DO NOT MISS THIS... He deemed that it was absolutely safe to entrust Himself to us, and did with utter assurance, for the ground that afforded Him an utter and a perfect sense of safety to do so was that He was giving Himself to us.

Woe to us. Woe to us. Woe to us.

For we are reminded that God cannot but be the greatest gift. And therefore, the greater the gift given... the greater the sense of safety afforded and personal assurance that it will be received and not rejected. Yet this also affords something else. For the greater the gift, the greater the possible sin if that gift is despised. Horrifically, in agreement with our forefathers, we assume this great guilt today by continuing to personally rebel by rejecting Him for lies originated from the Devil, despite the light of knowing what occurred, despite the light of a continual revelation of His person in creation, and for many... even despite the calls of His gospel of grace. Receive Me, don't reject Me! Receive me once again and I will forgive!

So much more sense the gospel makes in light of this being the central reason for the cross! For despite what has happened we are called again unto Him... we are called to return, through gracious means, to that which we have rejected: to value and cherish Him first and foremost in the midst of restored relationship where we have only previously shown either apathy or open contempt. Therefore in this gospel of grace we are to firstly be enlightened and reminded of eternal worth of what we in utter abomination and folly despised and forsook: God Himself. Secondly we are to not lose sight that a perfect display of love has been questioned, awesome knowledge and wisdom have been despised, and the commands of an infinite power rebelled against. But we are not to stop and merely wallow in despair. For in the newness of our conscience's submission in light of the truth, we are free now to lay down our arms, our utter hardness to the magnitude of the situation, and admit in all honesty our desperate need for His proportional remedy for our sin and our situation: Christ sent to us... and His life willing surrendered unto excruciating suffering, public shame, and death on behalf of our exceedingly great sin.

CHAPTER 8

MY NEIGHBOR IS WORSE THAN ME

"Pride gets no pleasure out of having something, only out of having more of it than the next man... It is the comparison that makes you proud: the pleasure of being above the rest. Once the element of competition is gone, pride is gone."

— C.S. Lewis, Mere Christianity

Reader be warned: because of how utterly distasteful I have personally found our next subject and the violence with which I have resisted it, I assuredly know many will choke, scoff, utterly disregard, or set aside as foolish the realities and truths that follow. Which is woeful because they are a great key and reason for our current sickness. Therefore we would do well to listen and fear when the Lord so speaks to us. For after all... His name is Lord and God.

****

What do many of us hate more than to be compared with, let alone equally labeled with all other sinners? "Utterly disgusting!" I of all people surely know: for I too once held myself very high relative to my 'lowly' and 'evil' neighbors, and I was so utterly assured in this position, that any proposal otherwise was so utterly distasteful and unacceptable that I would either choke or pass over what the Spirit said altogether. Therefore let the reader be encouraged to not avoid this subject should they hate it to the utmost as I have on the front end, and instead, meet it with humility and receive as we will be pointing to later, that a singular yet absolutely major piece missing from the church today and our own Kingdom experience, sorely needed, is bundled herein and waiting to be released and received by those who surrender their conscience to the truth of God.

Though I did not realize it, for much of my life I treasured nothing more than to compare myself with my neighbor. And why not? I was clearly praise worthy indeed. I excelled instead of failed at the things that I did. While my brother struggled, I was succeeding... or at least that is what I thought. Good grades, awards, the praise of my teachers and peers, honor, college, and the list goes on. And in regard to morality or how I conducted myself, I was altogether different than... and would not involve myself with shady characters... those who gave themselves over to their desires, drank, and the sort... or so I was convinced. Now stop and consider my mindset with me along with logical and necessary end it led me. I eventually was enlightened to how I was functioning: I surely thought my identity, self-respect, and relative greatness were both found in and best viewed through my own eyes in comparison with my neighbor, just as almost all of humanity and many believers continue to function today. And I would not have ever thought otherwise had not first the Spirit speak the gospel of Christ and shine the light of truth into my darkness and folly and address me otherwise, and I reach a point of such utter depravity that I could not hold to this image of myself any longer. Reader be further warned! This subject is met with such utter violence and disgust for these more specific reasons: our self-created identity, our misplaced personal value, and our carnal image of greatness are at stake and cannot coexist in light of such truths... but if you are willing to and do not run, we will soon see that the Lord has far greater in His open hand for us than that which we asks for us to surrender to Him.

****

It is the removal of comparison which we hate. Just as Mr C.S. Lewis has pointed out to us, when the comparison is gone so is much of our pride. Admittedly, pride cannot be fully explained by this definition alone, but it is very worthy and extremely pertinent to our current discussion. Let us make one last very important point about what we will be saying and what we will not be saying before getting started. We are not in denial of their being various types of sin. Nor are we in denial of the degree and scope of evil caused unto others and the Lord by various degrees of a sin. Nor are we in the denial that the Lord himself labels certain people groups as especially wicked. (Gen 13:13) But what we will be eventually saying is this: that there is genuine and undeniable grounds for us to no longer distance ourselves from our neighbor when it comes to our sin... the difficulty to submit to such a word from the Lord being a primary root of sickliness and an absence of grace and compassion among us. Therefore let us attend closely to such words, as much is at stake.

As our first point of a removal of comparison, let me remind the reader of a gospel subject already touched on by us which directly speaks unto this evil mindset. For some their evil desire proceeds forth from their heart, reaches their hands and mouth, and we visibly and audibly see that which they commit. Others keep it as clean as possible on the outside, but commit those same sins on the inside. Therefore the first removal of comparison aimed out our pride by the Spirit, which is easily understood, is that both have committed the same type of sin. One is adulterous on the inside and lusts after a woman in his heart, another actually leaves his wife for another woman. Yes there is varied evil caused, nor are we denying that we should be understandably more outraged at one... but both have the same evil desire in their hearts... the heart being our principle person. Therefore they seem different on the outside, but in truth share the same appetite on the inside. Notice, in addition, that we are not in denial that both have evil desire, and that it proceeds forth from our heart. (James 1:14) We are not blaming that which lies in our hearts on another or the circumstances. Therefore, the reader is firstly encouraged to stop abruptly and be circumspect in order to give up the lie that they are wholly different by perceiving the various ways the same evil desire manifests itself among men: the same desire hidden from others or manifest in various ways. We therefore must also acknowledge the sins and idols that we have likewise committed and worshiped which we have previously considered foreign, innocent, or free of in light of this fuller and utterly truthful picture. Yet, this alone does not fully explain or address such a subject adequately. Therefore we will be inquiring to two more major truths addressed to us.

Are we not different in many ways from our neighbor? Certain things are undeniable: height, weight, gifting, physical and mental capacity, our means, and the list can go on and on. So how then can pride or comparison ever be removed? God's intended health for us as Christ followers is not found in the removal of comparison when it comes to these subjects for we are intentionally created different by Him. It is instead found in the beauty of a full picture of why He has done so. If everyone was an Alastair Fray, I think I'd be quite depressed, for the beauty of the human race is often found in our differences. God has not intentionally made us different so that we can lord and boast about our differences and then spread our contempt on anyone who lacks that which we possess. God's image of the human race and in a smaller sense, those in Christ, is that of a body. Each piece of the body is different, unique, yet cannot not be removed from the rest and say that it is not needed nor without arrogance say that it does not need its other members. The human race and we as the church of Christ bear different skin color, languages, gifting, means, various skills and abilities, and the list must go on... and His charge to us is to respect one another as essential and valuable and serve one another in our differences just as each member of the human body does not deny the other but instead gives and contributes in accordance with its ability and function. Notice: this is a uniquely spiritual mindset, granted to us in light of the truth of how Christ has organized His members and in admission that the Spirit and God the Father has thus created man in His image. So stop your lording!... and acknowledge that all that distinguishes us has been given to us... or we have obtained to it by grace or by power, means, and time that God given. Thereby we will regain much of the peace of His kingdom come, a revitalized strength, and joyful cooperation in once again celebrating such a beautiful and truthful image of humanity and our brothers and sisters in Christ. "I see the beauty in the tones of skin"[27] What a wonderful expression of eyes enlightened by the truth of how God has both created us and meant us to live!

Before moving on I must acknowledge, that His name not be slandered, that most assuredly not all of our differences can be explained by God's direct hand or intent... for often the differences we see amongst ourselves are a results of living in a fallen and sinful world. Yet... this does not negate the utter value and absolute necessity of all of our eyes and minds being renewed in light of what the Spirit speaks to us about His glorious image and intent in designing us to live, support, and value others for their unique gifts and person... despite our weaknesses and infirmities.

****

I anticipate, should you have taken our inquiry

seriously and attended to that which has preceded with genuine care and thoughtfulness that you have found such things enlightening and extremely helpful in light of Who they originally came from. But the section that follows is the reason why this chapter is in this book. Therefore apprehend what He wishes to say to us:

So wherein lies the singularity of our sin? What is the undeniable reality which surrenders our ability to distinguish and distance ourselves from the sins of others? The Lord has spoken it to us again and again all throughout history and therefore we are without excuse. There are a myriad of passages that we could quote but we shall be drawing on the chapter and the specific verses of the bible that decisively broke my heart and revealed to me what in truth I was doing, and therefore ushered me back to the presence of the Lord:

> 'Return, faithless Israel,
> declares the LORD.
> I will not look on you in anger,
>   for I am merciful,
> declares the LORD;
> I will not be angry forever.
> Only acknowledge your guilt,
>   that you rebelled against the LORD your God
> and scattered your favors among foreigners
> under every green tree,
>   and that you have not obeyed my voice,
> declares the LORD.
> Return, O faithless children,

declares the LORD;
　　for I am your master;
I will take you, one from a city and two from a family,
　　and I will bring you to Zion. (Jer 3:12-14)

While originally spoken to Israel, we know as Christ followers that whatever the law and prophets speak is spoken to all those under the law of God... which is all men. Therefore in my sin, in our sin, the Lord speaks thus to us: "RETURN, FAITHLESS ISRAEL" "Return faithless Alastair" "Return faithless ____" The image clearly communicated to us again and again by the Lord throughout scripture and the prophets is that of a husband to his unfaithful wife or that of a father to his faithless children. And we are His faithless creations indeed. Therefore the singular label given to all sinners is: **unfaithful** (Luke 12:46). Therefore what is to gained from this?

　　Does not the Lord select His words carefully so that we realize in truth how we are and have conducted ourselves so that conviction of the evil we have caused and the reality of our sin come upon us? The reality that He wishes to impress on us is this: that just as a wife betrays her spouse and leaves him for another or a child betrays and leaves his family of origin... so too we have betrayed the one and only God and left Him. But for what reason do men stray and seek to live apart from God? The similarity is that they all stray and seek to live apart from Him because they believe the lie that they can find their hearts desire in things other than Him. One man strays to money, another to sexual immorality, another to power, another to an idol that promises what he most desires. The similarity is that all have strayed from God. And the cause? A proposed lie by the father of lies, Satan himself... leading to doubt, leading to an completely unwarranted slandering of a Holy God in receiving that lie, leading to faithlessly treating and leaving the living God to worship, live for, and pursue anything and everything but Him. **We are the faithless. We are the unfaithful. It is just a matter of to what, to whom, how far, and to what lie a person has strayed where the distinctions are made among us. And herein we find that we can no longer distance ourselves from our neighbor.** As promised, these things along with the faithless and hopeless state it produces are the eye opening view of man's sin that we said we would eventually revisit. The reader should therefore take serious note should they be genuine in their pursuit of God's righteousness or despairing in regards to a remedy to their sin which troubles and pains them, for God's remedy to faithlessness is a faith granted to us by Him. Much could be written and expounded upon here but it will have to wait for another day and another time. Let the reader be encouraged though, we will not so easily leave such a major subject, for we are wholly interested in both what lies at the root of our sickness and will expound on God's peculiar remedies.

So wherein lies the benefit of such discussions? Remember the Apostle has directed our attention to a good conscience being the grounds of the love that he aspire to see in us. We have in this section been pointing at an utterly prevalent pride which is the result of an evil conscience at odds with what the Lord speaks unto it. But what if we were to surrender? It is impossible for us to do justice to the grace and reach of such humility in light of the word of God but we will make an attempt at it:

Suppose a man who previously looked down at all the sexually immoral finally realizes sinful lust is also alive in his own heart and subsequently he confesses and finds forgiveness and grace in the midst of the recognized uncountable times he has committed adultery or sexual immorality in his heart. Would and should not the recognition of such shared evil desire and a mutual need for grace and forgiveness lead to compassion when confronted with another human who has instead committed the same desire on the outside by the removal and admission that they are not so different from one another after all? Or going even further... what if he recognizes that his lusts began small and grew to be worse over time and therefore it be but the same root in various degrees of perversion? Of what manner of understanding and compassion could he have for those who have the most corrupt and perverse forms of this desire should this slippery slope be acknowledged? Tell me: of what value is this realization and the resulting compassion and understanding to the church today and to all parties involved? Of what value to our society are a people with compassion and understanding yet do not deny evil? For we surely gravitate towards one extreme or the other, either excusing the sin altogether or bludgeoning our neighbor who's sin is as foreign to us as white sand is to a penguin. Yet let us continue. Suppose a man pride himself in the many things that distinguish himself from his neighbor and he let his neighbor know by distancing himself intellectually or socially from him or by voicing his open contempt for those who are not like him. Should he confess and admit his distinguishing characteristics are not the basis of his value nor are they the favoritism of God, but by His design to serve and love others... of what new manner of life has he received in light of the glorious truth God has placed in his heart? And still yet: Suppose a man has strayed from the living God to worship doing things in his own power as if the Lord had not given him such things. Though he see his neighbor who has likewise strayed from the living God, he can never meet him with compassion nor understanding for his neighbor worships ease and a lack of effort whatsoever. But suppose the first man, convicted in the light of truth, return to the living God and confess that he has namely been unfaithful and he recognize the truth that men have all exchanged God for a lie. (Rom 1:25) Has not God infiltrated the darkness of his heart and freed him through the Spirit of Truth and a genuinely new mind to now approach his neighbor who worships the lie of laziness and a lack of effort? Of what value are such things to the life of the church? Of what value is such compassion and understanding that reaches across all previously held barriers and prejudices in our society and our world? Truly! Stop and consider the implications of the gospel, this remedy of God. Racism cannot stand in light of such truth, nor can we live any longer as we have. I fear and perceive that the change be so great, yet so utterly worth what it cost, that those who see it will surely confess with the Thessalonians that "These men who have turned the world upside down have come here also." (Acts 17:6) Yet it is not in truth us first who will have turned the world upside down, for He has first transformed us through His word and by regeneration and renewal of our mind and thereby we speak what we have received and experienced by grace alone to others. (Eph 4:23) He has granted us eternal life, the life of Christ. Therefore lay hold of it and lay down your arms!

If despite our previous encouragements and the light of the truth you still find that dealing with such a subject and the association of ones sins with another carries the same distaste and utter disgust with which I first met it, let me give that person both a warning and an encouragement. Listen closely to what the Lord Jesus has to say unto you:

> For whoever would save his life will lose it, but whoever loses his life for my sake will find it. (Matt 16:25)

God is not asking you to deny the varied degrees and effects of individual sins. But for you to follow in Christ's steps you must lose and leave your former manner of thought and life. For to return to a person and Lord certainly necessitates leaving certain things once held dear behind. And He has called us from every which way we have strayed to return unto Him through the gracious death of His Son. Take this as a warning. For Christ intends it as such. For yes, it would be easy to hold to and continue to cherish your relative goodness... and it may seem like a ridiculous ask to give up something so precious which has formed our identities, greatness, and self-worth for so long. But be encouraged in this... He is out for your good. He does not take without adding or replacing something exceedingly greater and more satisfying. You must believe this to overcome. Where then does your treasure lie? Is it the kingdom of God or is it your pride? For the kingdom of God is like a pearl of great value which a man was willing to sell all that had to buy. (Matt 13:45) Let us then look at what He is in fact asking you to submit to. In light of these truths He is asking you to surrender lies, especially that which concerns our relative goodness and the distancing of how we have conducted ourselves compared to others, though this lie is utterly precious to us indeed. But stop and consider this: what have we lost in truth if it be but a lie? Therefore let us loose what we cannot keep to gain which we cannot loose for the life of Christ is found alone when we abandon our own righteousness and admit our need for His.[28]

CHAPTER 9

HERO OR VILLAIN?

Do you think of yourself highly or lowly? Do we, as a race, gravitate toward looking at ourselves as the good guys or the bad guys? For who among us, including myself, fantasized about being the villain vs. the hero? No... we put on the cape, dawn the breastplate, pick up our trusty weapon of justice and slay those fierce enemies of peace, justice, and all that is good and right!

If we are the hero's to begin with... why then do we need to be reconciled to God? Or in other words. How then can we even begin to receive a call from the Lord to confess our unfaithfulness and waywardness and return to Him through receiving of the grace of regeneration when I'm clearly on His team to begin with? This prevalent mindset finds most gospel truths, including those we have recently covered, both peculiar, foreign, and almost always preposterously offensive. Yet contrary to this mindset the word of God speaks thus:

> And you were dead in the trespasses and sins in which you once walked, following the course of this world, following the prince of the power of the air, the spirit that is now at work in the sons of disobedience— among whom we all once lived in the passions of our flesh, carrying out the desires of the body and the mind, and were by nature children of wrath, like the rest of mankind. But God, being rich in mercy, because of the great love with which he loved us, even when we were dead in our trespasses, made us alive together with Christ; by grace you have been saved. (Eph 2:1-5)

Time and again we are likewise spoken of as being a dead people, separated from the life of God, in need of a new birth through His life giving Spirit. Scripture therefore confronts us with a crossroads: Will we be offended and set God's words aside as if He doesn't know what He's talking about and continue to maintain that we are the hero… or will we have enough humility to admit we neither understand nor see everything that the God of the universe does? Dead in what sense? Desperately in need in what sense Lord?

If I may speak to it, the primary issue at hand in this confusing picture is that we have for far too long taken for granted and not understood the consequence that the Lord said would befall us if we sinned against Him by eating of the tree of the knowledge of good and evil in the garden of Eden. We pass over the story as if the consequence does not concern us today. But we are all Adam and Eve's children, we are their bone and flesh, and therefore it does concern us by familial connection. In love the Lord warned us that we would "surely die" upon eating of this tree. (Gen 2:17) Yet peculiarly we find the Lord is seeking them Adam and Eve out and having conversation with them after they had already eaten of the tree. Did they mysteriously avoid the consequence of death? Or is this death of a different kind: stunningly apparent when considered and carrying with it a complete lack of life and the stark contrast with the living that physical death illuminates?

It is for and only in communion with the Lord that we have been created. Therefore it is not for no reason that one of the two sacraments for Christians is the taking of communion. Therefore let us be informed: 1 Cor 6:13b "The body is not meant for sexual immorality, but for the Lord, and the Lord for the body." God's design and intention is that He indwell us by His life-giving Spirit through covenant relation with us. But... sin entering our prior relationship through us... and no small sin for that matter: a separation has occurred and unresolved sin stands between us. Let it be observed that the resolution of sin is necessary because God is just as He is merciful, His perfect hatred of sin just as true as his love for sinners... and therefore does not and will not excuse or pass over sin as if it is nothing. Having once shared relationship, we are now separated and "living" quite apart from Him. Yet many would contend that they are still quite on His team. Do we see the complete disconnect? So let us inquire into the various signs of a dead people, even if we currently object as I have.

Dead people, when looking at their thoughts and motivations, have no mindfulness for the person and relationship for which they were originally created... and what mindfulness they presuppose to be of worth to God does not resemble at all God's original image or intent for their relationship with Him. Of dead people, He says this:

> The Lord saw that the wickedness of man was great in the earth, and that every intention of the thoughts of his heart was only evil continually. (Gen 6:5)

'Every' is obviously a very strong word. I think most of us

would very quickly admit the deadness of a person who has no mindfulness for the God in who's world they live in and the relationship with Him for which they were originally made. Deadness in this respect is seen in the complete lack of activity whatsoever toward the Lord their God. But what about those who deem themselves a pretty good person? Or what about those who head up non-profits? Or even those who do many things which almost everyone would call good works done in the name of obedience to God? What about them? Now I know we are treading on sensitive ground. But to not disturb this ground is to not love our neighbor... for the life of the conceited, the self-confident, those that run faster and harder then everyone around them is as precious in God's sight as any other life. So... here we go!

This following question I must ask the reader to answer with complete honesty to address such a subject and make a sober judgment :

> Would you be perfectly content if tomorrow God died? Unmoved? Not care?

If you really care about your eternal well-being be honest with yourself for it is alone those who live with the Lord and experience His loving kindness that ultimately truly love the Lord and eventually learn to obey out of love. If you answered 'yes', 'yes I'd be perfectly content if God died': such an answer is in the very least a sure sign to you that your current obedience is almost completely unfounded on a loving relationship with the Lord and your experience is shallow at best though you may in truth be saved. Such people ought seek the Lord diligently for why their experience and obedience is so shallow and sickly for it is good to be certain of your placement and position. At very worst if you answered yes, this may be a sign to that you are still fully dead and God is but an afterthought and is in fact treated with contempt by you in true revelation of your inner conversation, motivations, and life. Therefore the deadly similarity between the religious, the 'good person', and the cause oriented solider is that none of them give a hoot about God. They remain faithless.

    What dead people ultimately need to understand, though they may not see it at first is what I needed to understand. Dead people are still faithless and hardened to the gospel of reconciliation. In other words, though they run, though they labor, though they seem superior in every way to their neighbor, all that they presume that is of worth to God that they have done or wish to present to God is rubbish. And why am I qualified to speak to such things? I have been a part of the group. Blessed with an excellent education. Excelling in the things I put my hands to. Honored among my peers. Running faster and harder than most. But all the while now in hindsight, abiding in death. Deadness toward and a lack of relationship with the Lord Jesus Christ is again the issue here since it is by Him and for Him that we have been created in the first place. Like "white washed tombs" it all looks fine from the outside, but inside lies selfish ambition, performing for others approval, satisfying our own self-image or pride, and a complete absence of faith or love that both honors the Lord is must be attached to the gospel. We maintain a lie before men, and pride ourselves in the lie. But will you presume to bring a lie before God and that He will receive it as a gift worthy of heaven?

Before proceeding to our next point let me give an encouragement especially to the saved for what has been spoken previously can and is meant to cause us to be uneasy, especially if we are lacking, but that unease should not undermine the truth of God's open arms. Understand that the life God is "as a mustard seed". The signs of His power in your heart and His life then may start as small as a mustard seed, but in time, as you trust Him, follow Him, and submit to Him, it will grow and overtake that which remains of your old self. Therefore if you are submissive, attentive, and pursuing the Lord, you need not fear... for He receives us and then works on us, not the other way around. In contrast, dead men do not have regard for nor are they appropriately affected by the word of life, the glorious and good news of the Lord Jesus Christ. They continue in sin and do not have a change of heart. They are not attentive to Jesus but may 'throw him a bone' every once and a while. And lastly, the most certainly aren't interested in the person and righteousness of God.

****

Unfortunately, scripture does not stop at describing our spiritual condition as dead. It goes even further. In view of our person apart from new birth the apostle Paul calls us all "children of wrath" and Jesus himself, seeking to shed spiritual light in the midst of darkness calls us "sons of the devil".

> For we have already charged that all, both Jews and Greeks, are under sin, as it is written:
>
>> "None is righteous, no, not one;
>> no one understands;
>> no one seeks for God.
>> All have turned aside; together they have become worthless;
>> no one does good,
>> not even one."
>> "Their throat is an open grave;
>> they use their tongues to deceive."
>> "The venom of asps is under their lips."
>> "Their mouth is full of curses and bitterness."
>> "Their feet are swift to shed blood;
>> in their paths are ruin and misery,
>> and the way of peace they have not known."
>> "There is no fear of God before their eyes."
>
> Now we know that whatever the law says it speaks to those who are under the law, so that every mouth may be stopped, and the whole world may be held accountable to God. (Rom 3:9-19)

And from Christ's words himself:

> You are of your father the devil, and your will is to do your father's desires. He was a murderer from the beginning, and does not stand in the truth, because there is not truth in him. When he lies, he speaks out of his own character, for he is a liar and the father of lies. (John 8:44)

These images and passages go far beyond our proclivity to explain margins of our life as sinful and the rest good, and instead, go so far as to label our very nature, our very core being, as being sinful through and through. To be under sin, as scripture says all men are, is to be under death. And the author makes it clear that it is unto all of us that these things are written. So far removed are these things from our high image of ourselves as it elicited and still elicits the most violent of opposition and revilement when it is impressed upon us:

> The Jews answered him, "Are we not right in saying that you are a Samaritan and have a demon?" (John 8:48)

A Samaritan being one of the most contemptibly held members of their society, and His words so unacceptable as he surely is possessed by a demon. Yet many, including His own disciples recognize this of Him despite their own doubts at His words:

> John 6:60, 66-69 After this many of his disciples turned back and no longer walked with him. 67 So Jesus said to the twelve, "Do you want to go away as well?" Simon Peter answered him, "Lord, to whom shall we go? You have the words of eternal life, and we have believed, and have come to know, that you are the Holy One of God."

Therefore, we too in view of knowing that He surely is Lord, God, and Christ… must not set aside that which He has said, but rather strive to see the truthfulness of His words and inquire into why He has thus said it.

During His conversation in John 8, our Lord Jesus, names certain characteristics peculiar to Satan. Of all the Devil's characteristics, He specifically names his murderous and deceitful nature. It therefore is logical, that if we are dubbed sons of the Devil, that we too carry these characteristics.

Already, in our previous chapter, we have addressed and begun to describe the sources of our peculiar proclivity as a race to look our neighbor and hold him or her in contempt. The signs of this are so far reaching and so abundantly obvious as we cannot exhaust all possibilities... but to name a few: one's political stance to another's, one's skin color to another's, one's manner of life to another's, and one's people group towards another's. Yet, this should be abundantly obvious to us, but is worth mentioning: our contempt is not contained solely in our hearts. It eventually reaches our mouth's, with which we destroy and harm of neighbor.

> "You have heard that it was said to those of old, 'You shall not murder; and whoever murders will be liable to judgment.' But I say to you that everyone who is angry with his brother will be liable to judgment; whoever insults his brother will be liable to the council; and whoever says, 'You fool!' will be liable to the hell of fire." (Matt 5:21,22)

It is not me who likens treating ones neighbor with contempt or as a fool to murder... It is God himself who does so. Yet, we don't stop here. Our contempt is not merely contained in our hearts, reaching our mouths... but eventually reaches our hands. We act on it and sometimes murder our neighbor. It is a road of progression... but identical heart. Therefore to be like Satan, we need not to have physically murdered our neighbor yet, but instead have any degree of it working out inside of us. In true consideration of such things... how guilty I am of this! Where Christ loves, I have discarded. When Christ hopes, I have written off. Where Christ seeks reconciliation and redemption, I secretly or loudly cry "Crucify them, crucify them, crucify them." Lord help us! While this does not sum up all the reasons for which we are murderous I have peculiarly singled this progressive tendency of ours out, for often at it's root is the sin of self-righteousness.

We have also begun our conversation, perhaps unknowingly, about deceit. If a life of death is characterized by sin, it stands to reason that attaining to true life, is characterized by righteousness, love, and faith. Yet, many pretend to this life, or even more, are convinced that they are living it whom our Lord calls hypocrites and white washed tombs. I, having been one of these, am a prime example. The key word here is "pretend". They deceive others, convince some but maybe not all of their neighbors, and even deceive themselves... just as I once did. And as an evidence of such, I present to the reader an evidence to the pervasiveness of this spirit, an all too common saying of ours:

"nobody cares anyway"

Living among one another, having experience after experience, in evidence of the facts of our daily lives and interactions, seeing past the show... we summarize the evidence, see past the pretense, and conclude that "nobody cares anyway". "Everyone" is just pretending. But how often do we find a person or ourselves admitting that "nobody" includes ourselves as well? Notice, that when our neighbor uses this saying... we are included in the circle. But when we say it, we conveniently leave ourselves out. That is how powerful this deceit and darkness is. We clearly see the mask, the pretense other's are putting on, but dare not admit or dare to look at the lie we are living, lest we loose what is most precious to many of us.

> "Some people are friendly, but they'll never be your friend. Sometimes this has bent me to the ground." – Rich Mullins

Let us be reminded at this point, that in beginning this discussion, the point of talking about and inquiring into such things is not that we flog ourselves and live in a permanent place of despair or self-loathing, or for this to be yet another means of treating one another with contempt, as some will do in contrast to the good news of Christ's love for us. But rather, that an evil conscience, unwilling to admit to how dire our situation is cannot receive the good news of Jesus Christ. Nor, can we as believers, already saved by Him, experience the heights of joy and depths of peace that the Lord intends we live in if we cannot appreciate or admit who we have been, and what He has given us by grace. As a reminder, it is for us to live in power, in joy, in freedom that I have undertaking writing. Thus we conclude that sin is not a marginal description of only a small part of our lives, but rather, such a pervasive power in view of pervasive contempt and pervasive deceitfulness as we can no longer resist our dead nature, being born of the devil himself. The distinctions found in how closely we resemble him (Matt 23:15), though we all resemble him in degrees until we are born of God through the resurrection of Jesus from the dead. I understand that such talk is wholly un-receivable to the natural man... but as previously stated, I have addressed this book namely to the church... those born of the Spirit and who will not leave His side though they find what He says hard to accept at first.

There yet remains the utmost aspect of our person's

before we are changed through receiving the gospel and sanctified by His Spirit which removes all doubt that we resemble Satan, just as a violent storm lays stubborn foundations waste. The revelation lies in our resemblance of the original sin of Satan himself. Satan, being a created angel, given gifts, personhood, power, and position from God, instead of honoring God and giving Him the credit, rebelled against God. Satan, despite all his enjoyments, laid eyes on that which he could never have… namely the place of God. It is with the very same temptation that he first tempted us in the garden:

> "But the serpent said to the woman 'you will not surely die, For God knows that when you eat of it your eyes will be opened and you will be like God, knowing good and evil." (Gen 3:4-5)

If I invite my friend into my home and share with him the gifts given me, shelter and house him in his need, share with him the food from my dinner table… of what response would expect from him? Gratefulness demonstrated toward me and appropriate honor before others of course. But if instead, my friend, upon seeing my wife, develops an evil appetite for that which is rightfully mine alone, and acts upon his desires in seeking to take that which he has not right to… would I not be rightfully outraged and full of perfectly good jealousy? We, like Satan, have a particular desire inside of us, apart from regeneration, for that which is rightfully God's alone. A particular thing that that in dull consideration of the circumstances, makes God justly outraged and likewise full of perfectly holy jealousy. Namely, a desire for God's glory: the seat and place in which

He alone is to sit in.

You see... it is not just a rebellion against a command. It is in fact treachery. A desire for the seat and place of The King, which is utterly disgusting in light of how great a gulf there be between us. Recall how we started our discussion in this chapter... how we envision ourselves. Do we envision ourselves as the hero or the sidekick? When it's all said and done, and the story is ended, are people clapping for us or for Him? You see, God is the hero, and no other conception of God is logical. Any other conception of the end, other than that given in Revelation, of Jesus being the clear hero and center, with the Father, and Spirit is evil. It's the very fact that many of us hate this prospect of an end that immediately reveals the heart of enmity. God being the origin of all things good, all our gifts, the power of our minds to create, the power of our hands to work, the origin of a new life lived with Him, and every other good thing we can possibly exhaust thinking of, therefore gets the glory. It's all rightfully His. Saying this is not a denial that God will ultimately honor those faithful with that which He has given them in Christ, but is rather a call that we cannot deny that we as a people have a dominant proclivity to act as if we are the origin or fountain of these things, and thereby directly resemble Satan, who being a creature, aspired to the place of His Creator. The athlete glories in his prowess and power, yet not in the Lord who gave him the gifts, opportunities, and means to develop these things. The student, comparing herself, glories in her superior intellect, not honoring the one who gave her the gift and opportunity to develop this in her life. The rich man, in view of his possessions, glories in himself and that he has accomplished his success by his power alone, never acknowledging that the power, time, and gifts given him by the Lord are that which enabled him to accumulate his belongings. God is dead in this mindset, and we are quite happy about the prospect.

CHAPTER 10

I'M WORTHY OF WHAT?

"Though I did not realize it, for much of my life I treasured nothing more than to compare myself with my neighbor. And why not? I was clearly praise worthy indeed. I excelled instead of failed at the things that I did. While my brother struggled I was succeeding... or at least that is what I thought. Good grades, awards, the praise of my teachers and peers, honor, college, and the list goes on. And in regard to morality or how I conducted myself, I was altogether different than... and would not involve myself with shady characters... those who gave themselves over to their desires, drank, and the sort... or so I was convinced." – Alastair Fray

To begin: what is the natural end of my above admitted mindset? By all measures against my peers I was certainly worthy of praise and had the accolades to justify it. The key word that connects with our consciences here is the word worthy. Our assessment of what rightfully belongs to us. Because, despite hearing the facts or hearing the gospel, many of us, including myself, have not properly assessed our situation... what we are truly worthy of. And our false or hardened assessment of our situation is in large part a root of the lack of spiritual vitality amongst us. Therefore... let us consider a few select examples of people whom our God greatly esteemed in light of their assessment of themselves and their subsequent faith.

To begin, Abraham himself makes an important jump of logic that we should obviously closely listen to in light that God himself has so highly honored him:

> "I am not worthy of the least of all the deeds of steadfast love and all the faithfulness that you have shown to your servant, for with only my staff I crossed this Jordan, and now I have become two camps." (Gen 32:10)

I would like to submit to the reader that all-important starting point of Abraham's above admission is an admission of personal unfaithfulness which was the most vital admission that we often miss talked about in the previous chapter. Starting here, Abraham himself then makes an important jump of logic that compels him to confess that he is not worthy of even the least of God's deeds of "steadfast love and faithfulness" toward him. But wherein lies his logic?

Steadfast love and faithfulness are experiential blessings namely in a relationship. But who and what situation could result in deeming oneself not being worthy of even the least of kindnesses from the other party? The most logical answer in consideration of others, and in consideration of what scripture speaks to us, is my first submission... that Abraham is not at odds with God and is instead wholly aware of his manner of life, wayward and unfaithful to Him. Only then does such an admission truly make sense, for who is unworthy of even the least of kindnesses from another person in relationship except the person who has acted unfaithfully. For instead of faithfulness or steadfast love... would not anger, justice, and a broken relationship be all that remains after such an act? Herein lies a key point of Abraham's logic and the reason why an act of unfaithfulness explains such an admission. Abraham see's what he is worthy of in light of his personal unfaithfulness and therefore marvels at the steadfast love and faithfulness he is experiencing. Therefore the pleasing admission of his good conscience owns to in truth how he has treated the Lord, sees in truth the anger and wrath that he is worthy of, but most of all confesses the goodness of God in saying that his experience can only therefore be explained by grace and mercy: that though he be not worthy of the least of God's deeds of kindness... he nonetheless has obtained to gracious relationship and steadfast love despite his deeds, through repentance, righteousness, and a salvation of God. We have much to learn from his admission... for this admission is also that which pleases God today and motivates the lives of those who recognize what they are receiving instead of what they are worthy of. And if God is so pleased with a good conscience it will do us well to listen to more admissions:

Faith Conscience and Heart

One of the Pharisees asked him to eat with him, and he went into the Pharisee's house and reclined at table. And behold, a woman of the city, who was a sinner, when she learned that he was reclining at table in the Pharisee's house, brought an alabaster flask of ointment, and standing behind him at his feet, weeping, she began to wet his feet with her tears and wiped them with the hair of her head and kissed his feet and anointed them with the ointment. Now when the Pharisee who had invited him saw this, he said to himself, "If this man were a prophet, he would have known who and what sort of woman this is who is touching him, for she is a sinner." And Jesus answering said to him, "Simon, I have something to say to you." And he answered, "Say it, Teacher."

"A certain moneylender had two debtors. One owed five hundred denarii, and the other fifty. When they could not pay, he cancelled the debt of both. Now which of them will love him more?" Simon answered, "The one, I suppose, for whom he cancelled the larger debt." And he said to him, "You have judged rightly." Then turning toward the woman he said to Simon, "Do you see this woman? I entered your house; you gave me no water for my feet, but she has wet my feet with her tears and wiped them with her hair. You gave me no kiss, but from the time I came in she has not ceased to kiss my feet. You did not anoint my head with oil, but she has anointed my feet with ointment. Therefore I tell you, her sins, which are many, are forgiven—for she loved much. But he who is forgiven little, loves little." And he said to her, "Your sins are forgiven." Then those who were at table with him began to say among themselves, "Who is this, who even forgives sins?" And he said to the woman, "Your faith has saved you; go in peace." (Luke 7:36-48)

This being our next passage notice first that Christ is bringing to light an assessment: namely the debt we have incurred as sinners. These debts must be dealt with for perfect justice and accounting is an essential and unchanging aspect of God's character. In view of evil the done, the harm, the taking, the pain... a debt is to be paid by the offending party to settle accounts. In this case Christ compares two debtors who owe two different amounts.

One 50 denarii and the other 500 denarii. In both such cases both could not pay. Upon being pleaded with He takes pity on both of them and cancels both of their debts. (Matt 18:26, 27) The primary oint of the above illustration from our Lord is to understand the connection between how much we are forgiven and how much we love the one who accomplishes our forgiveness. The more miserable the situation the greater the potential response from those forgiven and who experience grace is how it is supposed to work! Paul's description and personal experience of how this played out in his life and in others mirrors Christ's image: faith working through love (Gal 5:6). And how beautiful and great a picture we have of the proper response seen at the beginning of this passage in the actions of this woman who understood her sin! Having rebelled against the Lord of heaven and earth and having nothing we can give to Him which is not already His or due to Him in the first place we are in a horrible predicament. We must take a pause and appreciate this as Christians for we often forget such things in the midst of the continual grace we enjoy. It would have been fully good and just if God had made us pay for our sin against Him and against others. Yet we cannot and could not pay. So He pitied us for our situation was dire indeed. (Matt 18:27) But the person who has been forgiven little loves little. It is alone the person who has been forgiven much who loves much. Herein we find connection to our beginnings on a good conscience. For we began with an evil conscience that is in denial of the magnitude of it's sin and therefore the debts it has incurred. But in revelation of this passage our continued hardness then has done a great disservice, for it is in large part why we love the Lord so little and are so utterly unstable versus on fire. God's purpose in us facing the truth about our sin in all its ugliness and scope is not then that we wallow in it, but that in admitting the debt that is properly ours we may know and experience ourselves that the one who is forgiven much loves much! THE ONE WHO IS FORGIVEN MUCH, LOVES MUCH! Again, I am not in personal denial that the Lord and the bible speaks in various ways of degrees of guilt, but for us to deny the magnitude of our sin or how truly miserable our situation was for the sake of pride only steals from our experience of utter joy and overwhelming gratefulness in our experience of grace and in hearing the same words this lady heard from Christ towards us: "your faith has saved you, go in peace." Again is this situation we find that we must lose something to find something exceedingly greater.

> And he said, "There was a man who had two sons. And the younger of them said to his father, 'Father, give me the share of property that is coming to me.' And he divided his property between them. Not many days later, the younger son gathered all he had and took a journey into a far country, and there he squandered his property in reckless living. And when he had spent

everything, a severe famine arose in that country, and he began to be in need. So he went and hired himself out to one of the citizens of that country, who sent him into his fields to feed pigs. And he was longing to be fed with the pods that the pigs ate, and no one gave him anything.

"But when he came to himself, he said, 'How many of my father's hired servants have more than enough bread, but I perish here with hunger! I will arise and go to my father, and I will say to him, "Father, I have sinned against heaven and before you. I am no longer worthy to be called your son. Treat me as one of your hired servants."' And he arose and came to his father. But while he was still a long way off, his father saw him and felt compassion, and ran and embraced him and kissed him. And the son said to him, 'Father, I have sinned against heaven and before you. I am no longer worthy to be called your son.' But the father said to his servants, 'Bring quickly the best robe, and put it on him, and put a ring on his hand, and shoes on his feet. And bring the fattened calf and kill it, and let us eat and celebrate. For this my son was dead, and is alive again; he was lost, and is found.' And they began to celebrate. (Luke 15:11-24)

Our next opportunity to see a pleasing admission of the conscience is in midst of this ever relevant and well-loved parable. We will need to tie together a few lines of thought that we have covered thus far along with closely listening to his assessment he is worthy of. Let us admit and recognize that like the prodigal son, we have sinned against the Lord, left the relationship to pursue other things, and find ourselves in a heap of misery. Now in the case of the prodigal son we see him experiencing right shame for his actions. He also has made an assessment what rightly belongs to him, what he is worthy of: shame... not praise. Yet, the prodigal son goes even further than this. In light of his actions, he rightfully confesses that he is no longer worthy to be called a son. But on what grounds? How does this make any sense? To answer these questions... let me pose to the reader these thoughts: For what reason do we boast of our promotion and new title at work? Is it not because it is a badge of honor? And would I not be greatly honored if I were the son of the late Billy Graham? Why yes I would, for his last name alone, would honor me. Yet we have previously noted that the prodigal son has rightly assessed that a place of shame, not honor, is what he is due, in light of the nature of his sin. What many of us have not seen about our sin, including myself, is that it does not carry alone the implication of debt and punishment, but also shame. And therefore, since we are justly worthy of a place of shame in the sight of God, it is also therefore just for us to lose all titles and statuses of honor that we once previously held... honor being no longer fitting for the one who has sinned. The prodigal son recognizes his rightful loss of status and we too our loss of standing before the Lord our God: for having once walked with Him freely in the garden of Eden, we are now cast out, dead men, carrying a name of shame... sons of the Devil. And what is the place of shame? The place of sinners? It is non-other than the pit. Hell itself. It is unfitting for sinners such as ourselves to have any contact with the honorable... let alone the One and only God... who lives and is seated on an infinitely high throne not in a lowly place of shame. Therefore the prodigal son in approaching his father for mercy only hopes to attain to the status of servant in his father's house. Yet, to his surprise, his father receives him back: forgiving him, restoring him, and elevating him far above what he previously and rationally hoped for. This as well is our story if we submit to the truth... if we recognize and acknowledge the glorious ring of the Spirit of truth. Hereby such things, in recognition what we are truly worthy of, rightfully have lost, and our place, we are once again free to rejoice when we too are given grace so extravagant as it would bring any man confronted with it to his or her knees!

> Then I looked, and I heard around the throne and the living creatures and the elders the voice of many angels, numbering myriads of myriads and thousands of thousands, saying with a loud voice, "**Worthy** is the Lamb who was slain, to receive power and wealth and wisdom and might and honor and glory and blessing!" (Revelation 5:11-12)

CHAPTER 11

CONCLUSION TO A GOOD CONSCIENCE

I cannot emphasize enough how important it is for us to grasp the significance of a good conscience in the greater picture of spiritual life and health returning to us both individually and collectively as the church. So wherein lies the dividing line then between an good conscience and an evil conscience? For we began here for a reason... because we can no longer stand for such lack of spiritual understanding on such a vital subject, even if I have not done it full justice. But we have been enlightened unto the stark contrast between mindsets... for the previous distinctions made between an evil or good conscience were explained either by circumspect and humble submission or popular hardness to that which the good news of Jesus Christ speaks unto the mind, or further, by the same response to God's greater revelation in scripture. For what's wrong with a mind at odds with the magnitude of what has been committed but that it does not consciously admit it surely needs the infinite value of Christ's blood to save it from hell. Or what is wrong with a conscience that does not admit universal unfaithfulness except that it has not first closely listened to the Spirit through scripture or spoken word nor recognized that this is what it really is doing. And of our deadness, progressively worse murders, and the deceitfulness of our former life what shall we say? Notice, all of these belong to the light of the revelation of God which's end is surely His one and only Son, Jesus Christ of Nazareth... and thereby we see that a good conscience is only gained in true submission to the fullness of this revelation... and, is by grace alone: for we would not know such things nor would I have ever inquired further expect in true conviction that the Son has come and in the light of His person... for He alone is the way, the truth, and the light which gives light to all men. (John 14:6; 1:6-9)

By the above we find that grace whereby we can put to death that which remains in us after salvation. For indeed, it is grace... but we most assuredly are directed unto careful and skillful handling of such grace unto the end of us both putting to death sin in our bodies once and for all by those who are genuine about their return to God. (Rom 7:21-25; 8:13-16) But who still sins still but those who's evil conscience still remains? Or who is obedient and experiencing the fullness of the eternal life of God but the one who has humbly recognized the hardness of their conscience and humbly received the Lord the Spirit's remedy in the message and revelation of Jesus Christ. It's always a gospel remedy that saves us. It can only be a gospel remedy that saves us. For by no other design would the Lord save us but by His hand. Those that hate this image are those who still can't stand God being the Hero, the Center of the story this story. But how rebellious and evil is that in light of Him being the beginner of all things?

What is to be gained? For in light of the admitted difficulty we must firstly be reminded again that it is worth all that it cost us. For the reader and myself must be reminded and encouraged often that the kingdom is a pearl of great price, which is worth selling everything it cost in order to gain it. For the eternal life of scripture and God himself, seen aright, are of such greater value to us than that which we must leave behind that they are not worthy of being compared. (Rom 8:18-25) God is not a taker... He is a giver... and any image otherwise is slanderous and disingenuous to all manner of evidence and experience to the contrary. Furthermore, the benefits personally, corporately, and for our world if we confess the thoughts of our evil conscience and receive a new mind through regeneration and the light of God are staggering. Herein we connect with where we began the book. Our and others experience of a kingdom that has already come and an eternal life that has already been granted are so utterly shallow because we find ourselves still at odds with many of the most fundamental things that the gospel speaks unto our consciences. Let me ask then. For how much longer will the church stand if we continue to lack the heights of joy that are bound found in us truly together knowing the nature and magnitude of our sin and then knowing the gospel? How longer can we stand a luke warm life when we know there is a feast set before us? Shall the world and even confessed believers continue to clamor, discuss, and spend enormous effort to end racism and contempt without us applying the remedies of God? How long will it be until we and the church seek to understand and grasp universal unfaithfulness seen through the rejection of God himself for anything and everything but Him so that common understanding, compassion, and sense can return to us? The kingdom of God comes through the gospel of Jesus Christ alone. A kingdom of peace, of rest, of justice where we give people the respect and love they deserve. Of what value first to ourselves and to the furtherance of the gospel lies in us being able to explain deadness? For how can we explain receiving eternal life unless we see what was lacking in the first place? We cannot wait any longer or I fear for the future. Nor can we any longer despise nor handle foolishly the Lord's remedies in the gospel, though they have long been offered to us. The right responses, the right emotions, love, a good and upright life only come when we acknowledge and receive all of the gospel... not just pieces. We have been given the keys to the kingdom of heaven, but few are knowledgably and lovingly opening the doors. Therefore we now see a second reason why we are so sickly, for to still be largely at odds or lacking understanding or depth with that which we have heard from the very beginning cannot but result in an utterly unstable life. Admittedly, the issue may be we just have not understood fully what was spoken, or have been taught wrongly through misunderstanding or guilty ignorance. But would that we all once again grasp such things, for our experience of the kingdom and our joy is at stake, and the vitality of the church is inarguably connected with the prerequisite of a good conscience.

A PURE HEART

CHAPTER 12

DIVIDED ALLEGIANCES

In the sixth year, in the sixth month, on the fifth day of the month, as I sat in my house, with the elders of Judah sitting before me, the hand of the Lord God fell upon me there. Then I looked, and behold, a form that had the appearance of a man. Below what appeared to be his waist was fire, and above his waist was something like the appearance of brightness, like gleaming metal. He put out the form of a hand and took me by a lock of my head, and the Spirit lifted me up between earth and heaven and brought me in visions of God to Jerusalem, to the entrance of the gateway of the inner court that faces north, where was the seat of the image of jealousy, which provokes to jealousy. And behold, the glory of the God of Israel was there, like the vision that I saw in the valley. Then he said to me, "Son of man, lift up your eyes now toward the north." So I lifted up my eyes toward the north, and behold, north of the altar gate, in the entrance, was this image of jealousy. And he said to me, "Son of man, do you see what they are doing, the great abominations that the house of Israel are committing here, to drive me far from my sanctuary? But you will see still greater abominations." And he brought me to the entrance of the court, and when I looked, behold, there was a hole in the wall. Then he said to me, "Son of man, dig in the wall." So I dug in the wall, and behold, there was an entrance. And he said to me, "Go in, and see the vile abominations that they are committing here." So I went in and saw. And there, engraved on the wall all around, was every form of creeping things and loathsome beasts, and all the idols of the house of Israel. And before them stood seventy men of the elders of the house of Israel, with Jaazaniah the son of Shaphan standing among them. Each had his censer in his hand, and the smoke of the cloud of incense went up. Then he said to me, "Son of man, have you seen what the elders of the house of Israel are doing in the dark, each in his room of pictures? For they say, 'The Lord does not see us, the Lord has forsaken the land.'" He said also to me, "You will see still greater abominations that they commit." Then he brought me to the entrance of the north gate of the house of the Lord, and behold, there sat women weeping for Tammuz. Then he said to me, "Have you seen this, O son of man? You will see still greater abominations than these." And he

Faith Conscience and Heart

brought me into the inner court of the house of the Lord. And behold, at the entrance of the temple of the Lord, between the porch and the altar, were about twenty-five men, with their backs to the temple of the Lord, and their faces toward the east, worshiping the sun toward the east. Then he said to me, "Have you seen this, O son of man? Is it too light a thing for the house of Judah to commit the abominations that they commit here, that they should fill the land with violence and provoke me still further to anger? Behold, they put the branch to their nose. Therefore I will act in wrath. My eye will not spare, nor will I have pity. And though they cry in my ears with a loud voice, I will not hear them." (Ez 8:1-18)

Having first begun together shedding light on our generalized lack of a rooted faith today, along with our continuing hardness to that which we have heard from the very beginning, there still remains another very great reason why we are so spiritually sick.

In our society today, presuming as a whole that we have advanced beyond the base inclinations, foolish thoughts, and ways of our ancestors... we most certainly consider ourselves beyond the worship of idols. Though we are convinced, as many have so accurately and clearly pointed out by the grace of God, our thoughts and actions speak quite clearly otherwise. We may not admit as much, or even realize that we have been living and functioning likewise to date, but just as our ancestors... money, wealth, work, success, pleasure, and many other things were for them and still are set up as our security, as our means to happiness, satisfaction, rest, and the pinnacle of all we hope for and strive for. Therefore are we so different? Since we largely function just the same we would do very well to pause and listen to the Spirit's words, found above, spoken through the prophet Ezekiel... for in these words lie our last fundamental problem singled out by the apostle Paul: our pursuit, that which we love most, is still not God and what He offers. For we, being still under a lie that something or someone other than God himself will fulfill and bring about that which we desire, remain devoted and under the influence of 'vile images' though we belong to the living God. "If I just obtain ___ amount of wealth... then I'll be satisfied and at rest". "Peace and rest come from the avoidance and absence of conflict" Are we not clearly functioning just as our ancestors have? They may deserve though the greater credit, for they realized and named that which they worshiped... and we at large cannot. We are devoted... committed to obtaining that which we believe will fulfill our desire. They sacrificed to their 'gods'... we make numerous sacrifices at cost to us and others to pursue that which we believe will satisfy our desire. (Jer 2:13) They were a people characterized by devotion in thought, energy, and time to that which they thought would bring them that which they desired... we are likewise devoted, yet no longer a people characterized by devotion in thought, energy, and time toward the living God. (Matt 6:24).

So what then does it mean to have an pure heart? The passage from Ezekiel has been included for us to see that in the place where God was to dwell with His people, the temple, there was found that which is vile, detestable, and, for us to truly understand the Lord's disgust, He goes so far as to call abominations. In the place where He would expect worship to abide and exist, He found images worshipped in His place that provoked Him to jealousy... a good jealousy...

for He truly values our affections, attentions, and loves us, and therefore His jealousy reveals His value of our affections when either we willfully give such things to others, or another seeks to take away that which He cherishes, which is us... our mind, our heart... all of us! Let us in light of all we have discussed think of a pure heart in light of what we expect from our relationships. Do we not expect at our spouses attentions, affections, and use of their time reflect the single mindedness of their promise toward us and relation with us? In light of such common understanding, such an image of infidelity in the temple, of man leaving the one and only God to worship another, need not be so far removed from us, though it be spoken thousands of years ago. For their yet remains a temple today... where God dwells... unless we have forgotten?:

> Or do you not know that your body is a temple of the Holy Spirit within you, whom you have from God? You are not your own, for you were bought with a price. So glorify God in your body. (1 Cor 6:19-20)

And of His unchanging and continual desire for a single-minded devotion:

> Or do you suppose it is to no purpose that the Scripture says, "He yearns jealously over the spirit that he has made to dwell in us"? (James 4:5)

The greater warning there that must learn from scripture and again be reminded of is: in the hearts of believers, the temple of our body, in the place where the Lord God dwells among men today, the Lord still finds idols that provoke Him to righteous jealousy. (Heb 10:1; 1 Cor 6:19-20) God has entered the temple of our hearts with the expressed intent of being the only God worshiped there and therefore an the expressed intent of cleaning this house of all the vile things worshiped there. But is wealth still our security, pursuit, and joy? Is ease and comfort to be pursued at all cost? ... even unto the compromise and turning aside from following the God of all the universe? No other conception of salvation apart God's jealousy for having all of us and the abandonment of our images, that which takes precedence over God, should ever have been admitted by us. (John 14:23; Lk 14:28-30) Our hearts are not purely and wholly devoted to Him... and therein lies the crux of the issue and our adverb, 'pure', that the Apostle Paul is wishing to express to us... that... to love like Christ... we need to settle this conflict inside of us with whether we will wholly surrender, trust Him, and be fully devoted... or will we cling desperately to our images dominant our lives, produce bitter fruit, and continue our disability.

For this reason the following chapters are necessary. We have forgotten and lost sight of the greater picture of God's provisions in Christ that allow us to put such behavior behind us. We need to learn what of the Lord has been granted us to root out our old ways of living and enjoy the new, the courage and vulnerability to name what is vile and detestable in His sight, and learn how to deal with such accordingly. The results will be a newfound appreciation for the grace and power of this new life He has granted us, which does exist in power, and freedom to worship God and love others as Christ has called us. Therefore who or what dominates your life that you pursue and cherish above

Christ? This question must be asked of ourselves if we are to be even remotely honest about a return to the living God.

CHAPTER 13

GOD OF WEALTH

Wealth! Our security, our joy, our rest! That which we love most! We therefore cling to it. Fear sets in if we lack it. Should we feel compelled to share it our hand shuts and an explanation ensues. It is pursued at cost to our family, to our morals, at the expense of anything or anyone that would get in our way of attaining to it. Having attained to it, we create distance from others, especially those with needs, lest we feel compelled by the Spirit that we should surrender it. Begrudgingly we tithe. Begrudgingly we give. So where is the freedom I may ask? Or where is the power of God to save us from wealth's dominion?

Firstly, it is important for us to clarify that wealth in and of itself is not evil. Nor are we to give in every situation. But it is undeniable that we all are in particular danger of wealth becoming wholly unhealthy, even our god, therefore the Lord repeatedly warns us and gives instruction surrounding wealth. Consider then firstly the costs, sacrifices, social consequences, and bitter fruit of wealth as god: wealth as that which has taken control in our heart which now both informs our desires and that with which our minds are most occupied. These manifestations of such a rampant and common disease or condition are so self-evident as the reader is encouraged to pause and dully recognize them but they will not therefore require us to further expand upon them. So I will ask again: wherein lies God's freedom from this vile idol as his redeemed people? We remain conflicted. Our hearts are divided. We love wealth and hate Him. (Matt 6:24)

It is worth reminding the reader that I did not by my own power rationalize the Lord's remedy and prescribed freedoms from wealth that follow. In fact... it was quite beyond my ability or pay grade to do so. The usefulness of that which follows comes from honestly seeking to deal with revealed sin by depending on the Spirit of God, His truth, and expecting the grace of God in the midst of the process. The necessary place that we must start to address this disease is the tithe, which is absolutely clouded both in unhealth and misunderstanding for most people. We will begin by saying some uncommon things about it that are absolutely necessary for us to again perceive since such understanding has been largely lost in the church today.

****

The Tithe

I once thought that God's provision for us was only purely miraculous. In my mind His provision was only to be had through His miraculous power displayed by such examples like manna in the desert and bread and fish multiplied to feed many. Yet I was foolish and guiltily ignorant:

> You shall remember the Lord your God, for it is he who gives you power to

get wealth, that he may confirm his covenant that he swore to your fathers, as it is this day. (Duet 8:18)

In this verse a whole new context and concept of the Lord's provision was brought to light for me. This in the midst of a personal struggle to give the tithe joyfully. That which follows was never taught to me... though it has been in truth clearly known and recognized by men. The evidence of this being that thousands of years ago the above words were both spoken and eventually written. We understand by these words that God's provision is not to be understood merely by sovereign acts but also is explained by Him giving us the power to obtain wealth.

Consider with me: by what have we often attained to all we have? By our mind, our strength, our will, our talents and abilities, the time we have had, and the doors and people that have been available to us. Yet. Have we so forgotten and are we so blind as to who gave us all these? By virtue of creation.... none other than God himself! The issue or revelation to our lives at hand here and its application to the tithe is that many of us operate in a mindset quite contrary to this truth. Using the powers, opportunities, and gifts given us we accumulate wealth, yet have no recognition of God or His hand in the matter. The obvious results being neither have genuine thankfulness toward God nor any rationale on why we should worship God with our wealth. In the context of Duet 8:18, the Lord gives to his covenant people a land: excellent, fertile, and suitable to work... unto them being blessed. Yet... they are warned by Joshua, that once they have attained to that wealth, to resist the temptation to deny their God in not acknowledging that it is He who has given them this power: it is He alone who has opened the opportunity for them and for us to attain to our wealth and belongings. God has provided these things therefore what shall our response be? Shall we not honor and give thanks to Him? This is the lost logic of the tithe: a plain and logical recognition leading to natural thankfulness in light of who firstly gets the credit for all we have attained to. Into this context the tithe comes. Yet a danger still remains. For despite knowing the logic of the tithe we can still hate it.

Why then does He command that we give it? First and foremost let us recognize that the tithe is an invitation to trust in Him instead of in our wealth. For to give the tithe in a way that is pleasing to Him is to give it in such a way that demonstrates that we will no longer put our hope in or pin our security on wealth but in His power, on His watchfulness, in His love towards us, and on His promises. (Matt 6:24-34) Secondly, we must therefore give up the notion that God is out for 'our money'... or is manipulated by our giving. Both of these mindsets are offensive to God, utterly slanderous, and faithless. "God's a taker... watch your pocket book." Rubbish! "Don't expect Him to do anything for you unless you pay Him off." Anathema! Is God the most evil and profane father imaginable? Stingy and only motivated to act by being paid off? What utterly disgusting religion!!! And what a profanity in light of the gospel! For therein lies the issue with those who give with these mindsets. For they either do not admit the gospel or have not made the connection that their giving is to be done in faith, admitting the generosity, grace, and their standing in the gospel. His real generosity in the gospel and the glorious realities of our newfound relationship with Him are what lead us unto freely giving the tithe in a manner which pleases Him and are the key's He hands us to believe and thereby put wealth back in it's place.

To end things and be frank about my own life: the tithe is often where the rubber meets the road. Do I really trust Him? Is He really this watchful? Is He really powerful enough to address my needs or this situation? Is He in control and above my circumstances? Will I trust Him despite it looking bleak? Will I honor Him for who He has demonstrated He is and I have heard Him to be or will I pull back in unbelief? The tithe is freely and joyfully given by those who know who they are, understand what they have been given, and furthermore recognize who He is and has promised to be to us in Christ.

Sonship

Our next image of freedom from the God of wealth has much to do with our adoption as sons into the family of God. Horribly we know little of this freedom anymore, which speaks volumes about how poorly we have conceived of the gospel. The image is in fact an image that many of us are blessed to have known and experienced to a degree. This image of freedom is the image of a child who knows, that they know, that they know that their father loves them, and will not forsake them:

"Thankfully, my relationship with God took a major turn when I became a father myself. After my oldest daughter was born, I began to see how wrong I was in my thinking about God. For the first time I got a taste of what I believe God feels toward us. I thought about my daughter often. I prayed for her while she slept at night. I showed her picture to anyone who would look. I wanted to give her the world."[29] - Francis Chan

The fact of the matter is that our fears control us and lead us to try and find security in things or people, but most often in wealth. Our unrest leaves us ever wandering and ever pinning our hope again on things and people: the promise of our ability to rest being summed by how much is in our bank account or the means of the person our trust is in. But these never are enough so save us from fear nor the situations that can befall us. Don't miss this! The point is that: the child with a loving and perfectly faithful father who has a heart to give them the world and the arm to do so... should be... is... at absolute ease in the presence of their father. They alone can truly rest. They alone experience freedom from fear.

This speaks deeply to the freedom that is granted us in Christ Jesus. We must be convinced of who we are to Him, and who He is to us to experience the freedom of a child before a father. (Rom 8:16) For the point of Francis Chan is this: if he feels such for his children, how will he not expect the same and exceedingly greater from our heavenly Father. Mr. Chan is watchful and meets the needs of his children... God is greater, more watchful, and better at meeting our needs. Mr. Chan's heart is to bless his children... will we not see that God's heart is greater? Mr. Chan's children can experience peace, rest, and safety in the presence of their father... we can only know true peace, rest, and safety in the presence of the greatest Father. My hope is now the Fatherly appeals of the Lord unto us make much more sense, for He appeals to us with this logic: "If you then, who are evil, know how to give good gifts to your children, how much more will your Father who is in heaven give good things to those who ask him!" (Matt 7:11) And revisiting a previous passage to more fully know His heart:

> And he arose and came to his father. But while he was still a long way off, his father saw him and felt compassion, and ran and embraced him and kissed him. And the son said to him, 'Father, I have sinned against heaven and before you. I am no longer worthy to be called your son.' But the father said to his servants, 'Bring quickly the best robe, and put it on him, and put a ring on his hand, and shoes on his feet. And bring the fattened calf and kill it, and let us eat and celebrate. For this my son was dead, and is alive again; he was lost, and is found.' And they began to celebrate. (Luke 15:20-24)

The point is that He is greater... greater than any earthly father... and no other conception is logical... unless you be not convinced of His character yet. We are not alone. He is with us, and we with Him, if we have in truth heeded His call to return through His provided gracious means.

We therefore are to take the declarations of God's love for us, Fatherly heart, power, and watchfulness at face value. For we must become like children. (Matt 18:3) For freedom from wealth as 'god' and it's trappings is largely found in loving relationship and trust with a heavenly Father who has been gained through the blood of Christ. And we must not be like the Israelites in the desert who despite the abundant evidences of His love, faithfulness, watchfulness, and power... refused to believe and perished, never entering the promised land. (Heb 3:12-19) Mr. Chan would give his children the world. Our Father in heaven has already given us the world by promise. And if at the beginning of this newfound relationship the world be given to us and His one and only Son sent to us that we may have life, grace, and peace, how contrary and utterly crazy for us to not take up His invitation today to trust that He is willing, watchful, and capable to provide and is out to bless us in all His ways.

Labor in the House of God

Returned are we, returned to the house of the living God. While we have not as of yet physically returned we have neglected to realize that we have been granted the grace of living as such, for to be a child of God and therefore a part of a house is to enjoy certain privileges and potential blessings in places where we previous thought the burdens and situations were to be dealt with by us alone. In a house there is safety, the safety of a trustworthy Father's presence, assured generosity, intervention, and a hedge of protection even evil men put around their own. More so, there is love and understanding, present and expected love and understanding are alive in a perfect house, praise the Lord! Even more so, there is proximity. A household is about community, not an island of autonomy. Yet our spiritual and practical experience revealed by our fear and anxieties is quite to the contrary. We instead, perceiving that we cannot alone control our circumstances, the world, or our future, live anxious and fearful lives: lives constantly trying to hide or cope with such overwhelming realities. Lives grasping for and fabricating what assurance we can find. Or lives spent numbing ourselves to such realities in the hope anxiety and fear won't catch up to us. Alone, and without faith, far more resembling the Godless, we labor and scrape, neither expecting love nor understanding in the midst of a flood of labor. Without perceived title or home, we live as islands, without and sometimes in contempt of the community of a house. Yet these things ought not be so.

In truth, many of us no longer work for our fathers house as many once did, or work for the king of the land. But this is the reality of the new status we have been conveyed into: we can both serve a King or and live by faith and experience in the sight of a good Father. Be reminded then that both a King and Father will increasingly entrust a son or daughter with work to do. There is a gospel invitation and opportunity for freedom here that we have long since missed that stands in opposition to the bleak picture that we previously painted. For previously, we worked for earthly masters and served dark principalities and powers which only left us more empty and weary if you have indeed realized and confessed how you have behaved. But in contrast, to work for the Lord is freedom. He respects our limitations, unless you cling to an evil image of Him as a horrible task master and let Satan compel you otherwise. (Ex 3:7-10) We can now seek first His kingdom and serve Him with an assured expectation that He will provide for us and bless us. (Matt 6:25-33) God has concern for His servants, those who labor for Him... He most assuredly has concern for His children. (Ez 29:17-20) We can seek righteousness even in the face of a loss of wealth for He promises to provide for us. (Matt 6:25-33) All these things point one direction. There is a newfound freedom that can be peculiarly found alone by those who first recognize their newfound titles before God and secondly recognize and begin trusting Him as being greater than any earthly employer. For we are the "sons and daughters of a King."[30] We therefore do not labor as if He owes us, for our activity, our titles, and our life lived before Him is a gracious gift. (1 Cor 3:5-7) But to experience such freedom we absolutely must learn to take the step of faith that He has prescribed for us in this season in order to learn and see that He is trustworthy, is able to meet our needs, and even honors many of our deepest desires and fills one's we didn't even know that we had as we labor in and for the house and kingdom of God.

Before progressing on let me make a few last important points about wealth and God's image of freedom. Firstly, a further awesome and gracious aspect of laboring in and being a part of a home is being a part of a community and the relationships within that home. God has graciously conveyed us into a family! God's provision and image of care for us must then be recognized within the context of the relationships he has given us, especially those within the house of God. When we have fallen short of our own obligations, when circumstances which we can't explain arise, or even when God in His providence has allowed us to be in want it is often these people who step into the situation, but this is God's provision just the same, for the people He has created and the relationships He has granted. As a second observation notice when it comes to labor for and in a house for a father or king, in both images God's well-known and well-taught wisdom on the stewardship of our finances is not despised and set aside. In fact it instead finally finds its appropriate place in the greater picture of what God has done. For God does want good stewards, but we cannot forget that he is firstly concerned and pleased alone by faith, thereby intending for us to experience a unique freedom from wealth by entrusting our current and future well-being to his care instead of continuing in our anxious labor done in the hope of a rest that never comes. Therefore firstly, if we neglect or despise His wisdom and thereby steward what He has given us poorly, we should not then expect to attain to or retain the richness that He has given and intended for us nor experience His rest and peace, for surely His purpose in entrusting these things to us was in part for them to be handled and grown by His wisdom. But also, secondly, we are then to never, as I unfortunately did, take the wisdom of God on stewardship and then act like our stewardship is all that factors into the grand equation of our provision and security. For our story is in truth one of grace, from beginning to end, and anyone who wishes to boast otherwise ought to be ashamed of such a ghastly response to what God has truly done in their lives. For the revealed wisdom of God by which we handle our wealth wisely is but the grace of a good Father to his children. So His children are never to forget from whose mouth these things first proceeded and therefore they were instructed, nor forget that to have a Father is to experience a hedge of protection, real provision, generosity, and freely given gifts given simply because you are His child. Until we learn to recognize Him and therefore trust Him as both Father and King, fear and the dominance of wealth will remain. But for those who first know who they are and then look beyond their belongings to the invisible God, abundant freedom is their heritage today and forevermore!

CHAPTER 14

THE IDOL OF COMFORT

If we take a step back together and carefully consider our desires and pursuits when it comes to comfort, rest, and peace, we undoubtedly will find today that the typical Christian's mindset toward where to find such things far more resembles our culture's then the Lord's. "Comfort is to be had in that which I see" "Peace is the absence of conflict." "If I could just get away from all these problems and people... then I could rest." How these lies and mindset play out or look like in the individual may vary widely, but the same lie often is at the center of it all. These mindsets lead us to all manner of Christian compromise, evil, and lives lived stuck in this kingdom or world vs. lives lived for the kingdom of God which most assuredly has come. We pray as He taught us "thy kingdom come" but have lost the image, aspiration, and therefore desire to see that kingdom come. God is not enough for us and therefore our hearts are divided, impure, troubled, and anxious.

An Earthly vs. a Heavenly Mindset

Our absolutely necessary starting point that begins to release us from being unhealthily caught up in this present world is us personally receiving and recognizing that there is a greater reality which we cannot see. Are issue as Christians is not that we don't recognize this to be true but that we have not truly stopped to understand the it's implications on our present lives. Therefore let us understand: this greater reality intersects with ours often, for our world and all that is in it, including ourselves, was born out of the greater. (Gen 1 and 2) In addition this greater reality is of incorruptible substance and therefore is eternal and therefore is of greater substance than our reality. It is more real therefore and important on these grounds: it is eternal while this universe is temporal; it is indestructible and perfect while all that we see is corruptible and imperfect; that which is obtainable to in it will last forever while that which we have on this earth God has vowed to destroy.

> Too often we've been taught that Heaven is a non-physical realm, which cannot have real gardens, cities, kingdoms, buildings, banquets, or bodies. So we fail to take seriously what Scripture tells us about Heaven as a familiar, physical, tangible place.[31] – Randy Alcorn

Our beginning point if we are to have any hope of being free in this world is this: we must get rid of our cartoon fantasies and foolish thought about what our eternal dwelling place will be like and start listening to what the word of God really says about such things. The beginning logic then is this: both our world and the spiritual have substance, both our world and the spiritual are inhabitable, we can obtain to honor and wealth in either, but the former will not last along with all that is in it, which includes our belongings, our bodies, and even the world itself. No wonder we are so stuck. We have no mind for what will last. For belongings here may bring me pleasure, and God may indeed bless me with them, but to only work for and obtain to that which will pass away, whether that be title, honor, land, or wealth, without a mindfulness of our eternal pleasure in heaven, is a fools errand. We then must first personally and corporately return to a lush and vital understanding and perception of what lasts, the spiritual, if we, including myself, are ever to have hope to be free to live for a greater, more permanent, yet unseen reality. We have almost wholly lost sight and appetite for the original gospel message which is not alone 'the gospel' (the good news), but is 'the gospel of the kingdom of God' (the good news about the eternal kingdom of God)... which is not alone a present and advancing kingdom as we have stated, but is also a kingdom to come of indestructible substance and therefore of eternal worth instead of temporal worth to those who obtain to it. (Matt 9:35; Mark 1:15)

I'm have convinced that my personal experience when it comes to knowing scripture but it's practice being 'lost in translation', especially when it comes to reward, is in fact common experience. The disconnect between us hearing about eternal rewards and this actually having even the slightest bearing on our weekly routine being a perfect example of our knowledge of what Jesus has said vs. it's actual practical application in our life. This disconnect, lack of understanding, and folly is furthermore seen in our complete lack of appetite for eternal reward and almost no awareness of what treasure we have already obtained to. Therefore let us listen again to our Lord but with new ears:

> Do not lay up for yourselves treasures on earth, where moth and rust destroy and where thieves break in and steal, but lay up for yourselves treasures in heaven, where neither moth nor rust destroys and where thieves do not break in and steal. For where your treasure is, there your heart will be also. (Matt 6:19-21)

Observe: it is not then those who 'think' or 'suppose' they have treasure in heaven who's hearts are set on heaven, it's those who KNOW they have treasure there. This all goes back to our initial point: that we are stuck in this world and must admit that we are having real difficulty in shifting our minds toward heaven. Therefore to know that we have treasure in heaven we must first see the logic for ourselves. Only then, once we have perceived the Lord's logic, we can awaken from this earthly slumber and live lives that reveal that our hearts are set on heaven! For we will either be actively laying up treasure on earth or we will be laying it up in heaven, our hearts will be set on earthly things or they will be set on heavenly things with no other option inbetween.

> Blessed are you when others revile you and persecute you and utter all kinds of evil against you falsely on my account. Rejoice and be glad, for your reward is great in heaven, for so they persecuted the prophets who were before you. (Matt 5:11-12)

> Jesus said, "Truly, I say to you, there is no one who has left house or brothers or sisters or mother or father or children or lands, for my sake and for the gospel, who will not receive a hundredfold now in this time, houses and brothers and sisters and mothers and children and lands, with persecutions, and in the age to come eternal life. (Mark 10:29-30)

> And whoever gives one of these little ones even a cup of cold water because he is a disciple, truly, I say to you, he will by no means lose his reward. (Matt 10:42)

> According to the grace of God given to me, like a skilled master builder I laid a foundation, and someone else is building upon it. Let each one take care how he builds upon it. For no one can lay a foundation other than that which is laid, which is Jesus Christ. Now if anyone builds on the foundation with gold, silver, precious stones, wood, hay, straw— each one's work will become manifest, for the Day will disclose it, because it will be revealed by fire, and the fire will test what sort of work each one has done. If the work that anyone has built on the foundation survives, he will receive a reward. If anyone's work is burned up, he will suffer loss, though he himself will be saved, but only as through fire. (1 Cor 3:10-15)

Don't miss the Lord's logic! It is not for no reason that he says: "on my account" or "for my sake and for the gospel's sake". For these things phrases directly imply that the Lord objectively and clearly sees what it costs us to follow Him, what we suffer and endure because of being identified with Him, and that which we do for His kingdom's sake and that which has this appearance but is secretly done for other reasons. The logic is this: just as He has planted in our hearts a sense of justice or fairness toward those whom have suffered on our account or served us, He too will honor those who have been faithful and suffered thus. Suppose I do not show up to a scheduled lesson for a flute student of mine, but they have already paid for all their lessons in a month. Does not our God given sense of justice speak to us that "they have lost this time on MY ACCOUNT". Likewise the Lord who has a greater sense of justice than us sees that these have served "ON MY ACCOUNT". These have suffered "ON MY ACCOUNT". These have given "IN MY NAME". God sees, God does not forget, and God has promised time again to that He will recognize, honor, and reward. So now we know the logic of gospel rewards, yet fear remains that clouds and causes us to avoid this teaching even still. Therefore it must addressed before we can move on.

The fear that we speak of lies in the recognition that we have a peculiar proclivity to take pride in what we do and become wholly conceited. Therefore we avoid teaching about reward thinking that to teach such is also to promote conceit and a selfish motivation. But this is not so for those who acknowledge God's grace.

Our God is a God of justice: meaning those who deserve the wage of sin, which is punishment and dishonor, will receive it unless that punishment and shame be absorbed by the Son of God on their behalf. What then logically follows is those that deserve the rewards and honor of faithful service and sacrifice will also thus receive it. Pause at this point though to remember our previous discussion on our horrific loss of status and spiritual death unto becoming sons of the devil as a consequence of our sin. In turn, also recall at this point that we have through the grace of the gospel been restored and received as friends, sons, daughters, citizens, ambassadors, and people of the living God. Now, with these things in mind let us confess that the fear in many of our hearts, that to teach a mindfulness and motivation of heavenly treasure is also to promote unhealthy and selfish grounds for our obedience, is not justifiable! For... observe that those who are not in denial of their previous identity as sons of the devil and wholly dead are not in danger of such erroneous thought, for the life they live now as a child, as a citizen, as a friend, is but by the grace of God! For which of you by his or her arm forced the Lord to forgive them? Or how can we even live as obedient children, friends of the living God, the service of a soldier, an ambassador, or citizen, if we are not thus given such a title and gracious opportunity for that position in the first place? The solider, the friend, the child may all deserve honor, and they will most assuredly enjoy it, but if the opportunity and actual means of obtaining to our position along with the ability to live as such be but through the death of another our place, we have no reason to be conceited. Hereby these truths we are reminded that to have a heavenly or eternal mindset along with the expectation of reward is in fact firstly a gift, fully dependent on our salvation. Even so, God does not overlook the sacrifice that it has cost us to follow Him, that which is "ON HIS ACCOUNT", and therefore He is also not in denial of the real choice that we must make between faith and unbelief, to follow Him or to continue trusting in ourselves.

Lastly, if you suffer, but for the wrong reasons, don't expect reward and honor when you meet the Lord. For those who suffer and give for the wrong reasons, who have not love, though they even go so far as to give their bodies over to be burned, will not profit, will suffer loss, or may even be eternally dismayed. (1 Cor 13:3; 1 Cor 3:10-15; Matt 7:21-23) So get the gospel, it's mind and it's motivations, straight in your heart before claiming to have reward in heaven.

Peace as the Absence of Conflict

We began where we should have, the necessary movement of an earthly mindset toward a heavenly mindset, for why would we give up our comfort or even go so far as suffer if we are not firstly fully assured that eternity awaits us and that there is heaven, eternal reward, and honor to gain. These things being said, there often remain large obstacles between the reality of situation and a genuine willingness to no longer avoid or run from what Christ calls us to. Our next problem is that our concept of peace far more resembles our culture's than the Lord's. More specifically, we have bought into Satan's lie that the avoidance of conflict and the subsequent isolation of ourselves from even our own problems, our families problems, others problems, and the world's problems equates to our peace and rest. But it never does and never will. Let us then take a closer look at how this lie often plays out in our personal, interpersonal, and corporate lives lived in this world.

If the avoidance of conflict and the isolation of ourselves from problems is seen as the path to rest and peace we are most certainly individually doomed spiritually, for to follow Christ is also inevitably to invite real conflict, first and foremost within ourselves. The born again Christian will inevitably find that a real conflict of desire now exists inside of them, between choosing faithlessness or sin or choosing faith and obedience. But if we are either not yet convinced of the benefit we will receive if we follow Christ's command despite it's costs or yet remain wholly allergic when it comes to the difficulties of the path of life, avoidance follows and we consistently choose faithlessness and sin instead of faith and obedience. The issue for this 'Christian' is they have both not yet headed Jesus's repeat warnings about the costs and difficulty of the path ahead of them should they choose Him but more importantly in this matter, are yet unconvinced that facing their internal struggle between their sinful desire and obedience, faithlessness and faith, will result in their peace and rest. (Lk 14:25-25; Mk 8:34-38; Is 61:1; Lk 4:16-21; John 10:10) Furthermore... that those who are thirsty for lasting rest and peace will find it and thirst no more. (John 4:1-26) The conflict of ideals then is this: will you go on believing the lie that avoidance, isolation, and ultimately one's disobedience both has resulted in and still will result in your rest and peace, or will you surrender to the truth, that only those who listen to, follow, trust in, and therefore obey the Prince of Peace have the hope of and display personal and lasting peace in their hearts? The path to personal peace then therefore is riddled with conflict for our faithlessness and therefore sinful desire, which has led to our unrest and a lack of personal peace, must be remedied and put to death. But the root of sin is often not so easily remedied, but often comes with certain discipline, difficulty, discomfort, and pain.

Before passing on, there is a second reason why the idol of the avoidance of conflict lies is complete contradiction to the gospel. For those who repent, those who return to the King of King's and Lord of Lord's, will certainly find themselves in conflict with the prince of this world: Satan himself, his minions, and those under his influence. What then necessarily follows the reception of a Lord, the reception of a King, or to become a part of an expanding kingdom in largely enemy controlled territory, is assured conflict. Therefore the lasting peace which the Lord offers is contrary to our image of peace, yet a far greater peace in every way, for it is a peace that cannot be taken from us and lasts despite becoming richer or poorer, in sickness and in health, through testing, and quite despite conflict and danger. Therefore those who accept the discipline of the Lord, know His promise to them, and increasingly learn to trust Him despite the clamor and testing to believe otherwise eventually voice the confidence of the Apostle Paul: "For I am convinced that neither death nor life, nor angels, nor principalities, nor things present, nor things to come, nor powers, nor height, nor depth, nor any other created thing, will be able to separate us from the love of God, which is in Christ Jesus our Lord." (Romans 8:38-39) For quite despite their circumstances he and King King David are confident that the love and therefore the peace of God will follow Him them wherever they go. (Psalm 23:6) For the presence of the Lord cast out their fear. (1 John 4:18) And they have found that in truth, "all ways of the Lord are peace". (Proverbs 3:13-26)

Interpersonal

If all the ways of God are peace, why then do we not have peace in our relationships? The logical answer is that we are either not listening to the Lord or, just as in our personal lives, we are under the control of and in love with a false image of peace.

When it comes to our interpersonal relationships, the idol of the avoidance of conflict is particularly devastating for it often means we neither resolve our conflicts, nor speak our mind, nor speak up when we should. The results in our lives and others being obvious: for never having a conversation with our neighbor and therefore never resolving nor dealing with conflict and sin in a godly way, our relationships suffer greatly; in addition, in us valuing a peace which is no peace at all, we set aside our feelings and wisdom valuing a false peace before perceived and potentially real conflict with our neighbor; and lastly, we remain wholly allergic and therefore unwilling to step in and have the hard conversations with our neighbor, our friend, even our own family members that we already know should happen, choosing again a peace which is no peace at all above even our own flesh and blood. The idol of the avoidance of conflict therefore is and remains one of the most particularly devastating idols at work in America today. But why would we call it an idol? Why potentially elevate it to this level? The reason for this is, just as in our personal lives, this is picked before listening to Jesus himself. For just as the rich young ruler found it difficult to value Christ his comforts and leave that which Christ specifically called him to leave so that he may obtain to eternal life. So we continue to struggle today. (Matt 19:16-22) Likewise for us it is impossible to hold to the idol of the avoidance of conflict and continue to follow Christ in our personal lives and most certainly in our interpersonal lives.

For Christ has clearly said to us that "if you are presenting your offering at the altar, and there remember that your brother has something against you, leave your offering there before the altar and go; first be reconciled to your brother, and then come and present your offering." (Matt 5:23-24) Yes, I must acknowledge that many who do not seek reconciliation and therefore obedience to their Lord have a pride issue, but it remains that for many of us the fundamental issue is rather that we just can't stand to have the conversation for fear and anticipation of the conflict.

Wherein lies the freedom and hope in our interpersonal lives for the one who recognizes that this is their fundamental issue? The fundamental issue that we can address today for this person is that their mind is fixated on and simply cannot get past the perceived and potentially real conflict should they have this sort of conversation. The gospel answer for this person that is a major piece of solving the puzzle of our continued disobedience when it comes to conflict is that we must shift our focus off of the conflict itself and look past it toward the goal and end of the conversation. In the case of reconciliation or a particularly hard conversation we would look past the potential conflict of the conversation in the hopes of reconciliation, rest, and the peace that it is intended or will accomplish in our relationships or in another's life. Herein is the key then again that we must see: true peace and it's image, which proceeds forth from the mouth of and the gospel of the Lord, lies often in contradiction to our assumed image of peace and the worldly image of peace. But if yet cannot even reconcile and have healthy conversation even within our own family or the church itself, what hope is there that we will ever personally or corporately as believers affect our world as the natural outflow of the gospel working in our lives? Therefore do not neglect these three things. Firstly, recognize that the 'peace' that you hold to IS NO PEACE AT ALL! It has not nor will ever result in peace nor rest in your life for it is a lie firstly received from the father of lies, Satan himself. Secondly, recognize, assuredly meditate on, and thereby learn through meditation and practice that all of God's ways, especially when to how we are to conduct ourselves interpersonally, are peace. Thirdly, recognize the conversations that you need to have and when you are given the encouragement that you are ready to have the conversation, do not fixate on the conflict, but learn to look beyond the conflict to the reward, the end of why we are called to have that conversation in the first place!

Public

This idol of comfort and avoidance is a particular trap for us as Americans for it is easy fall into when within our borders we enjoy relative prosperity. In other words: in a land full of pleasures it is easy to worship pleasure and the absence of conflict and therefore we are warned. (Duet 8:11-14) The results of avoiding the issues at large within or borders or even outside our borders should we have the capacity and call to address them being obvious.

So how do we get beyond our ideas of peace and rest

and begin to face the problems within our communities, cities, borders, and world? We must begin with a correct view and appetite for where peace truly comes from. The Lord being the origin of every good thing, peace, true peace comes from Him and from following His ways. And it surely does... for those of us who have experienced salvation, who walk with the Prince of Peace, experience it! Where fear and anxiety used to dwell now security and restful assurance are finding root. Where enmity reigned He has brought peace, resolution, and forgiveness firstly for us and then in our relationships. Peace is the fruit of His Kingdom and therein lies the key. As we experience His power, relief, and follow His principles of peace it is then we find and see that for peace truly to come, His kingdom must come. The peace we have settled for is no peace at all for to make peace with the world and avoid conflict is also to set oneself against God. Our 'peace' is in fact war. The issue remains that the perceived conflict or our lack of security in the Lord both loving us and that He will never leave nor forsake us instead freezes us in situations where we are to be ambassadors of His Kingdom come. The key for many of us again is this: that we need to stop looking at the conflict and start seeing His invitations as peacemaking. For Christ ran into all sorts of conflict, but also taught us that "blessed are the peacemakers for theirs is the kingdom of heaven." Is then Christ a hypocrite? No He is not, for the conflict that He chose to have was in the pursuit of peace: for the man, for the culture, and for the world. It is high time the idol of avoidance as a means to peace is exchanged then for a true view of where peace comes from: first by our own entry and experience of peace through the Lord and then unto all the earth by an insatiable appetite to see this Kingdom come in others' lives and in our culture instead of making ourselves enemies by trying to make peace with our world and it's injustices. (Luke 2:14; James 4:4)!

Freedom in the Presence of God

We have at this point looked at two different grounds of leaving our comforts and our ideas of rest and peace: both a view of eternity and a new and clearer view of rest and peace. But humans cannot naturally give up our desire for rest, peace, or safety, nor does the Lord wish us to try and kill or deny our desire for such things. Therefore, to close this section on the idol of comfort, if we are to not fabricate or own version of these things where shall we satisfy our desire?

Let us be clear: God is asking you to uproot your falsely placed trust, in your creaturely comforts, in money, in your spouse, in whatever it is that you have pinned your hope on and we are to instead give it to Him. For consider where the idol of comfort, falsely place trust, and the lies you have received have led you? Your integrity has been compromised, peace is not found, and what rest you hoped to attain to has flown away. We have falsely placed our trust in that which could never supply our desire. Therefore it's high time we confess our sin, ask for forgiveness, and all get up and place our trust in where we can find it. Lasting peace, rest, and safety are found alone in the presence of the Lord. And this is where we deviate from all other religions... for our blessings are not achieved... they are given and found in a relationship that we have been given the privilege of living in. It is Him and Him alone, God himself who is the gift. In His presence, seeing who He is we find the satisfaction of our desires.

Yes, we may have hit on this before but we can't emphasize the image enough for those who are to have any hope of functioning and living different will greatly benefit from seeing the new image of comfort. Seeking the help and wisdom of my brother in Christ one day he directed me towards this image to address my fear, for fear is often the reason why we seek comfort in things:

> When one of my daughters has a bad dream she enters our room, crawls up under the sheets next to me, and falls asleep next to my side. Now think about such things Alastair. It's my presence that makes her feel safe, at peace, at rest. – David Cox (2013)

The point is God is greater in every way to my friend. Faithfulness, trustworthiness, generosity, and love. God has created, designed us, and identified himself as a Father in part so we may know Him through this familiar image of a father and his daughter. It's when we begin to know who He is, His perfect character and all this entails, and begin to trust Him with equal if not greater trust than that which we would give to our own father or another is when we experience the satisfaction and resolution of our desire. We can't fake it when it comes to this type of faith and trust for if we do not trust Him thus, we inevitably will find we will be sinfully and disappointedly trusting in something or someone else.

Let us end by saying that we should expect conflict for the Kingdom of God is opposed to the kingdom of this world. We are reconciled sinners found now in largely enemy controlled territory. For His kingdom to come therefore implies conflict. But we now enter conflict in a spirit of peace making, for we increasingly see that for peace to reign we must face our own inner conflicts, hard conversations must happen, and Jesus must reign in the hearts, minds, and world of men.

CONCLUDING THOUGHTS

CHAPTER 15

CONCLUDING THOUGHTS

Seeing the a greater picture of what undergirds our spiritual life is why I have written this book in the first place. Now that we have discussed the Apostle Paul's subjects we in hindsight can make necessary comments and conclusions as to where we should personally spend our time and see the much needed changes that must happen within the church and our personal lives for us to regain health and a strength of life that the Lord has granted to us.

Consider then: of what strength and stability of life would you expect from someone who has indeed both submitted their conscience to what the word of God says about their sin and condition, is likewise mindful to keep their heart pure, but yet has little to no root when it comes to being convinced of historicity of the gospel? The person is not filled with the undeniable and pressing reality of Jesus, the Kingdom of God, and His death and resurrection. How easily can this person be uprooted? Tossed to and fro? Can we ever expect them obtain to the fearlessness of the first disciples without the historicity of the gospel being rooted in their hearts? Or let us rather suppose that a man is both convinced of the historicity of the gospel and is indeed mindful to keep his heart pure but has of yet not submitted his conscience wholly to the Word of God: submission and admission that that which is spoken about his sin, his condition, and what he deserves is true, just, and right. Of what vitality of life or love and to what degree of response would we expect of the one who both does not admit how serious the situation is and therefore cannot appreciate the cost of the gospel nor the grace given him? Or lastly, suppose a man be both convinced of the historicity of the gospel and he indeed has submitted his conscience to the gospel but he is not mindful and vigilant to keep his heart pure. Though he have room to rejoice and he be thoroughly convinced of the Kingdom, eternity, and a Savior he yet remains duplicitous and divided, and therefore unstable, impure, continuously conflicted, and compromised. My hope for you and for us is that by this point we have both perceived and have received the indispensable and utter importance of the subjects the Apostle Paul has brought to our attention in 1 Tim 1:5: sincere faith, a good conscience, and a pure heart. For a present eternal life worthy of our undivided attention has indeed been granted to us, but it's foundations have long since been despised, neglected, and almost altogether forgotten. But these things need not be so. For if we with regained sight and renewed appetites restore these things first in our own minds, then in our teaching, and lastly in our churches to their rightful place, I am convinced we will experience a revival by the grace of God that has not been seen for generations!

APPENDIX

PRACTICAL ADVICE AND WISDOM THAT ARE WEAPONS FOR YOUR ROAD AHEAD

To follow Christ is not easy. It in fact is often costly. And the road itself is often seems both dangerous and impossible. Therefore I would like to share a few items that have been indispensable, items that I could not have been without lest I be overcome with fear or disbelieve unto the inevitable end of turning back or away from following the living God.

The first of these is one that we have already covered. That when we are confronted with an actual cost of following Christ we must be reminded in those moments and in that season that God is not a taker, He is a giver. For God has so loved us that he has sent His one and only Son that whoever believes in Him shall have eternal life. (John 3:16) A life worth selling everything for that we may obtain to it both today and forevermore, no matter the cost. (Mark 8:34-38) This often then comes down to an issue of faith. Though the cost seem too great, and the road be one we have never, will we still walk forward and open our hand being convinced that He is both good and has far better for us?

Nextly, let us acknowledge that that which is asked of us often looks like a burden far too heavy to carry. This most assuredly has been grounds for many to turn aside from following Him and is sure ground for a duplicitous life where we have put up barriers surrounding what He can and cannot have access to in our hearts and in our lives. In contrast the Apostle John encourages us and reminds us through his own experience following Christ:

> For this is the love of God, that we keep His commandments; and his commandments are not burdensome (1 John 5:3)

Furthermore, in contrast, the Lord beckons us to himself through this famous call:

> Come to Me, all who are weary and heavy-laden, and I will give you rest. Take My yoke upon you and learn from Me, for I am gentle and humble in heart, and YOU WILL FIND REST FOR YOUR SOULS. For My yoke is easy and My burden is light. (Matt 11:28-30)

But how contrary are words and notions to our current experience and feelings about what is being asked of us? What must be kept in mind when faced with things that seem too burdensome to carry is that God has created a way to indeed carry them but them to actually feel light. Obedience was never meant to be a chore nor are we left to face these mountains on our own. For is this not what we see in the gospel accounts and Acts? For the disciples and apostles followed Jesus at great cost, but were able to do so joyfully... not begrudgingly or with hearts that constantly pined for their way of life. The disciples and apostles also suffered greatly but never lost their encouragement, hope, or joy. The point that cannot be overlooked is that these things are indeed impossible for a man left alone but are not in fact not impossible for a man caught up in the promises and pressing reality of the gospel, eternity, and the Lord himself. There therefore yet remains a spiritual life to be lived, free, unburdened, and unhindered by the fears and concerns that control the lives of carnal men if we so admit the power and effectiveness of God's salvation on men such as John and Peter who previously could not stand. Remember then to not despair and turn away when confronted with burdens to heavy to handle but instead continue forward being convinced that He has provided and will provide for those that seek it out the means for you to easily and joyfully carry such things that previously looked impossible to carry or bear.

Lastly, we must be both vigilant and utterly convinced that the source of all life, that which we desire most, is from and can be found in God alone. For there is an enemy out to steal, kill, and destroy both us, our families, and our friends.

> Do not be deceived, my beloved brethren. Every good thing given and every perfect gift is from above, coming down from the Father of lights, with whom there is no variation or shifting shadow. (James 1:16-17)

Satan's tactic has not changed from the garden. If He can deceive you and thereby convince you that rest, satisfaction, honor, riches, joy can be found in something else or through someone else other than God himself then He has won the battle of your mind and you will inevitably fall and experience the loss and destruction he intends in your life, family, and in others. We must therefore ask for the grace of seeing and being utterly convinced that lasting peace, rest, and the satisfaction of our souls cannot be found any other place but in the presence of, in relationship with, and in the midst of faithful living with the living God, His one and only Son, and His Spirit that resides in our hearts.

ABOUT THE AUTHOR

Alastair Fray was born and raised in beautiful Seattle, Washington. Upon receiving his Bachelor's from the Eastman School of Music in Rochester, New York he began teaching music professionally. He and his family currently live happily in sunny Dallas, Texas where he has continued to teach. Among other things he is interested in the outdoors, playing the flute, and most of all quality time with his wife, adopted son, and family! Faith, Conscience, and Heart is his debut as a writer and publisher.

REFERENCES

[1] C.S. Lewis, *Mere Christianity*, Book II, chapter 2, "The Invasion," page 36

[2] John Owen, *The Holy Spirit: His Gifts and Power* (Ross-shire, UK: Christian Focus Publications, 2004), 176-177.

[3] John Owen, *The Holy Spirit: His Gifts and Power* (Ross-shire, UK: Christian Focus Publications, 2004), 176-177.

[4] John Owen, *The Holy Spirit: His Gifts and Power* (Ross-shire, UK: Christian Focus Publications, 2004), 176-177.

[5] John Owen, *The Holy Spirit: His Gifts and Power* (Ross-shire, UK: Christian Focus Publications, 2004), 176-177.

[6] Komoszewski, Sawyer, Wallace, *Reinventing Jesus* (Grand Rapids, MI: Kregel Publications, 2006), 75-82

[7] Komoszewski, Sawyer, Wallace, *Reinventing Jesus* (Grand Rapids, MI: Kregel Publications, 2006), 70.

[8] Komoszewski, Sawyer, Wallace, *Reinventing Jesus* (Grand Rapids, MI: Kregel Publications, 2006), 71.

[9] *William Mitchell Ramsay*: Wikipedia: https://en.wikipedia.org/wiki/William_Mitchell_Ramsay 7/6/17

[10] William Mitchell Ramsay, *Saint Paul the Traveler and Roman Citizen* (New York: Putnam Sons, 1904), 7-8.

[11] William Mitchell Ramsay, *Saint Paul the Traveler and Roman Citizen* (New York: Putnam Sons, 1904), 2.

[12] William Mitchell Ramsay, *Saint Paul the Traveler and Roman Citizen* (New York: Putnam Sons, 1904), 2.

[13] William Mitchell Ramsay, *Saint Paul the Traveler and Roman Citizen* (New York: Putnam Sons, 1904), 4.

[14] William Mitchell Ramsay, *Saint Paul the Traveler and Roman Citizen* (New York: Putnam Sons, 1904), 8.
[15] William Mitchell Ramsay, *Saint Paul the Traveler and Roman Citizen* (New York: Putnam Sons, 1904), 21-22.
[16] William Mitchell Ramsay, *Saint Paul the Traveler and Roman Citizen* (New York: Putnam Sons, 1904), 5.
[17] William Mitchell Ramsay, *Saint Paul the Traveler and Roman Citizen* (New York: Putnam Sons, 1904), 6.
[18] William Mitchell Ramsay, *Was Christ Born at Bethlehem? A Study on the Credibility of St. Luke* (London, UK: Hodder and Stoughton, 1898), 36.
[19] William Mitchell Ramsay, *Was Christ Born at Bethlehem? A Study on the Credibility of St. Luke* (London, UK: Hodder and Stoughton, 1898), 40.
[20] William Mitchell Ramsay, *Saint Paul the Traveler and Roman Citizen* (New York: Putnam Sons, 1904), 6.
[21] William Mitchell Ramsay, *Was Christ Born at Bethlehem? A Study on the Credibility of St. Luke* (London, UK: Hodder and Stoughton, 1898), 5-6.
[22] William Mitchell Ramsay, *Saint Paul the Traveler and Roman Citizen* (New York: Putnam Sons, 1904), 87.
[23] William Mitchell Ramsay, *Saint Paul the Traveler and Roman Citizen* (New York: Putnam Sons, 1904), 373.
[24] William Mitchell Ramsay, *Saint Paul the Traveler and Roman Citizen* (New York: Putnam Sons, 1904), 8.
[25] William Mitchell Ramsay, *Saint Paul the Traveler and Roman Citizen* (New York: Putnam Sons, 1904), 2.
[26] *Afford* (Merriam Webster Online Dictionary; https://www.merriam-webster.com/dictionary/afford) 1/28/19
[27] DC Talk, *Jesus Freak: Colored People* (ForeFront Records, 1995)
[28] Jim Elliot, *quote* (Wikipedia:

www.en.wikipedia.org/wiki/Jim_Elliot) 6/5/19
[29] Francis Chan, *Crazy Love* (Colorado Springs, CO: David C. Cook, 2008), 55.
[30] Tony Evans, *Kingdom Men Rising; quote* (Lifeway Films, Tony Evan Films, and Lot35 Productions, 2019)
[31] Randy Alcorn, *Heaven* (Carol Stream, Il; Tyndale House Publishers), 15.

Made in the USA
Middletown, DE
08 August 2019